BASKETBALL FOR BEGINNERS

GLOBAL
PUBLISHING
GROUP

Global Publishing Group
Australia • New Zealand • Singapore • America • London

BASKETBALL
FOR BEGINNERS

The Complete Guide for
Parents and Coaches
to Give Kids Their Best
Start in Basketball

Coach: Mark Anthony Walker

First Edition 2019

National Library of Australia
Cataloguing-in-Publication entry:

Basketball For Beginners: The complete guide for parents and coaches to give kids their best start in basketball - Mark Walker

1st ed.
ISBN: 9781925288636 (pbk.)

A catalogue record for this book is available from the National Library of Australia

Published by Global Publishing Group
PO Box 517 Mt Evelyn, Victoria 3796 Australia
Email Info@GlobalPublishingGroup.com.au

For further information about orders:
Phone: +61 3 9739 4686 or Fax +61 3 8648 6871

I dedicate this book to every kid that ever-dreamed Big Dreams and wanted something better in life for themselves and their family. As parents and coaches, I believe we need to focus on creation not competition. Let us build the skills, understanding and character of the kids in our care and give them the tools to live a truly great life by teaching them to chase their dreams and be resilient to the many challenges they will face. Bless everyone who invests time in our future generation, I thank you for making a positive difference in our world.

Coach Mark Anthony Walker

Acknowledgements

Mike Baker – rated one of the top three junior coaches in the country back when I started playing basketball. He was my first ever basketball coach who taught me so many basics in such a short period of time, instilling in me the values of hard work, discipline, teamwork and most importantly an increased desire to learn. Mike learnt how to coach basketball from a group of kids who gave him a book and asked him to teach them and one of these players went on to captain the Australian Olympic team. Mike was such a giving coach, often picking players up or dropping them home from training and games in an old blue van. A truly wonderful coach and man.

Sheryl Kaufman – my wonderful partner in building two very successful basketball programs from one to 36 teams in five years, as well as my own club from two to 90 teams over the last 18 years. Her tireless work has always been for the benefit of the kids in the programs and her passion for the sport and dedication to our parents, players and coaches. It is with much love that I thank her for everything she has done and is still doing for the club.

Les Gel – another coach who had a profound influence on my life and passion for basketball. He saw my transition from junior player to senior player at the tender age of 14 and I worked alongside with him building a new elite basketball program in central Melbourne. I spent 14 years as a coaching director building it from two to 36 junior and four senior teams. Les died tragically of a cancerous tumor a few years into building the program and I was proud to call him my friend and mentor.

Jay Brehmer – an influential coach who was one of the best training coaches I ever had as an elite player. He was a coach with a rich history and an incredible story teller. When he died his partner, Enid gave me all his coaching materials and I learnt many valuable techniques from Jay not so much for beginners but more advanced basketball techniques.

Past and Present Players – of the thousands of players I have worked with and still working with in many forms of the game, I have a huge debt and gratitude to them all. Some do test and frustrate me at times, but more importantly they teach me many values of patience, creativity, discipline, lateral thinking, providing a good example and more importantly inspiration to increase my skills as a coach.

Past and Present Coaches – for over 40 years of my involvement in the sport I have been cultivating my philosophies through coaching and being coached. Coaching is a great passion in my life and just like working with players I have had so many enriching relationships and opportunities to learn. Not all the experiences were positive, but even with negative experiences you are shaped to discount things that are not productive. I never stop learning so thank you coaches and God bless all of you.

Brodie Walker – my wonderful daughter who I spent many fun times with as she was growing up out on the basketball courts. She is a great coach at my club and also mentors our many young aspiring coaches and has given me so many wonderful memories. My deepest love and respect for a great person who is making valuable contributions in the lives of many kids.

Bonus Offers

Thank you for investing in this book!

To complement the book, I will be releasing a DVD series on basic skills to help parents and coaches along with our simple system and also drills to assist in running training sessions and teaching methods.

As a special gift to my readers, use the code BfB20 on purchase and receive 20% off.

www.TheBasketballEdge.net
www.GlobalBasketballCommunity.com

To help both player and coach and player we have partnered with Fast Break Sports to provide individual items and the economical packs to get you started on the right path.

Beginner Player Starter Pack
- Indoor/outdoor Basketball
- Reversible training tops
- Basketball shorts
- Basketball Socks
- Playing uniform
- Basketball Shoes
- Basketball Backpack
- Indoor/Outdoor Basketball
- Drink Bottle
- Basketball Warm up Top/T-Shirt

Coaches Starter Pack
- Polo Shirt / Hoody – Embroidered Logo
- Bag – Embroidered Logo
- Coaching Tactic Board
- 2 X Leather Basketballs
- 10 plastic cones
- 5 flat discs for spot shooting
- Whistle

Contents

DIAGRAM KEY

(1)   Offensive Player

(2)   Defensive Player

(C)   Ball

○   Coach

▲   Cone

↗   Direction Line

↗   Passing Line

↗   Dribbling Line

⇗   Shot

⊤   Screen

PREFACE

Welcome to *Basketball for Beginners*. After 28 years as a professional coach working with so many levels of basketball, I decided it was time to write a book. Basketball has been a major part of my life's work in the sport that I have an absolute passion for. Now people tell me everything that you could ever need in basketball coaching and development of players and teams has been written and yet this can never really happen. The human race is in a constant state of change, forward momentum and development and this is my contribution to an important generation, our children. Every kid deserves the very best that life has to offer and it is my intention that this book be the best possible guide for new players and coaches along with parents who certainly have a vested interest in the health, happiness and achievements of their children. This simple step by step guide for parents and coaches of new players will turn them into a productive team in a short period of time, and will be a valuable resource which I'll continually update and keep evolving. For the last 28 years, I have been coaching the very age group you may be involved with right now. Coaching and developing children aged from five to eleven can be a difficult job for any coach, let alone a young or inexperienced coach and especially a parent with limited sporting experience who really wants to help their child. I have several aims, the first of which is to keep as many kids playing the game for as long as they possibly can. Basketball is truly a dynamic game that teaches an individual so much and being part of a team in itself brings great life lessons, social skills and the body movements and hand-eye coordination involved can help an athlete in so many other sports. The game is a very fluid game requiring athletes to make several decisions on every play phase, thinking on the move is a skill in itself that can be challenging to master. Every parent out there wants their child to have a successful life in whatever activity they are involved in and sport plays are major role in many children's lives, especially boys but I am happy to say so many girls are now involved also. I love to see children have success and feel good about themselves and this book will certainly help you with their practice of basic skills and learning to play the game. It always warms my heart to see active parents getting out on the court with their kids and sharing the experience of the sheer fun of playing the great game of basketball. The best time to help your child will be early in their sporting years because at some point dad and/or mum your influence erodes and shifts towards the coach, stars of the game in the NBA or local elite teams and peers who become the kings and queens in a child's development as a basketball player.

You may be a parent thrust into the coaching role because you played a few seasons of sport as a kid. The fact that you have played sport in the eyes of some of the other parents can make you by default the most qualified. Now you have two challenges, one, coaching a team of beginner players and two, maintaining your own parent/child relationship. Older siblings and young players from the same club with very little playing experience are often coaching these teams. These young coaches are sometimes left to cope on their own with little support especially if they're not a part of a large club or their club has very little in the way of knowledge or leadership. Believe me I have seen it all over the years and this book is my contribution that will be helpful to all inspiring coaches as it will cover everything you need to build your team into a solid functioning unit. Even experienced coaches with quite a few seasons under their belt sometimes find themselves running out of ideas, lacking motivation, feeling stagnant and frustrated. You may even be an elite coach who is fantastic at working with elite players, putting that polish on them needed at that level, yet lack the skill and experience with younger beginner players. As a coach, I have felt all these emotions at one time or another and several years ago I started the process of using **KEY WORDS** in my coaching to accelerate the development of both player and team. Now all coaches use some key words during the game out of pure habit and I did also. I was getting frustrated with the rate or lack thereof, of improvement with my Under 10 beginner teams. It was then I started using **KEY WORDS** at all our training sessions linking these to the game. It was a simple enough system but made an instant impact. Most teams in my country get only 45 minutes to one hour a week to train and then play their one game a week. This is barely enough time to teach the simple basics of the game, and if there is a long break in between training and games it makes this task even harder. Kids and some adults for that matter can forget things very quickly and if there is a three to five-day break between training and playing the games you sometimes feel they are going backwards as a parent and coach.

All my Under 10 teams ideally train one or two days before the game and this simple switch of training nights helps with memory retention, keeping lessons learnt fresh in their minds come game day. Words can be so powerful and as a coach I used so many and wondered why it was taking so long to get what I thought was a simple message across. In my most frustrating times as a coach, I was constantly seeking better ways to improve the teams I was working with but not really making much progress, nor was I helping the younger coaches at my club in any real sense. In the midst of this difficult time as a coach I had a major breakthrough and it was a visit to an elementary school where I noticed teachers were asking the students to spread out by placing their arm on the person in front and to the side. For years I had been screaming out to the kids to spread out and wondered why this was such a hard concept to grasp and as a matter of fact I hear so many coaches in so many leagues almost begging their young chargers to do the same thing. This experience at the school was the start of my **KEY WORD COACHING SYSTEM**. It became the major element to taking a group of kids from pretty much zero to Team in eight weeks and this system will rapidly develop your team into a functioning unit in a really short period of time also. The system is very simple and it involves drilling your players with key words at training then using the same key words during the game. Try and replicate everything done during the training session and the players will respond accordingly (this is not absolute remember we are dealing with six to eleven-year olds). A simple example is that most Under 10 games are crowded especially around the ball. Like bees to honey these young players all want to be near the ball. Several years ago, the team I was coaching, on one of those inspirational days was involved in over 30 plus jump balls in a 36-minute game and I came away from this game frustrated as a coach, and for the players and supporters on the sidelines. It was then I put some serious thought into tackling this challenge (some people would call this a problem) and I started asking myself some interesting questions.

1) **Why do these kids continually crowd the ball?**
2) **How can I get them to spread out and create good spacing?**
3) **Once they are spread, what's the next step?**
4) **How can I condition athletes to respond instantly when we gain possession of the ball?**
5) **Can I teach it so a player as young as five years old could understand it?**

There had to be a simple solution to the five questions above and it was after much thought and reflection and the visit to the school I decided to drill the players with a simple **KEY WORD** called **SPLIT**. Basically, no player could be within four to five meters of the ball or another teammate, and this creation of space opened the game up allowing plenty of opportunity to advance the ball and penalised an opposition team that would not match up but was ball chasing instead. The next time we met the same team in competition I had been drilling the **SPLIT** for at least seven weeks, needless to say there were only six jump balls all of which we forced on our opponents with a considerable margin in the score in our teams favour, where the previous result was barely any baskets scored by either team. The margin was over 20 points in our favour and the opposition was still in the habit of crowding the ball which made things far easier for our defence. This one small adjustment to our training and the creation of a new habit transformed the team in so many ways suddenly it was far more fun to play as every player got involved.

The **SPLIT** helps rid players of bad habits, and one bad habit that really irked me was when players stood still, screaming the name of their teammate with the ball over and over to no advantage. With a sense of humour, I'd say to the players that surely their teammate actually knows their own name, so yelling it at them 500 times a game is a waste of energy which I'd rather see them use to **SPLIT** into space. Once they began to master this habit, they soon realised the opposition was still in the mode of chasing the ball with multiple defenders so by running forward of the ball they understood the **SPLIT** created easy opportunities to score. The **SPLIT** was only the start of the journey and soon many other **KEY WORDS** were introduced and utilised to great effect and this has been a huge part of my coaching philosophy now for the last 15 years. It has been a challenging journey but it has certainly been a huge part of the success my club and its players have achieved over so many years which still continues to this day. With all this in mind I see so many coaches and parents who have my greatest respect for helping these young athletes, yet give them very little in the way of direction and guidance. Coaching should be a wonderful journey, not a chore where you end up miserable or frustrated. You can help young players improve so much in a short period of time and take great pride in giving kids skills they can use their whole life. I am always filled with great pride when I see kids that I coached at the very beginning of their sporting careers now grown up young men and women, some even have kids of their own. There are doctors, lawyers and so many other professions and some have even come back to coach at my current club. Never underestimate the impact as a coach you can have on these young people, lessons learnt and simple disciplines can and will serve them well for the rest of their lives.

> *"It's what you learn after you know it all that counts."*
>
> - John Wooden

CHAPTER 1
Starting Points

CHAPTER 1
STARTING POINTS

Everything in life can be summed up by starting and finishing points and it is so important to remember that we all come from so many different experiences. Players will come into the sport, not just with the obvious physical attributes of height and athleticism or lack thereof, but with so many different levels of coordination and also interest in basketball. Some will come from elite sporting parents, others from parents who had little interest or involvement in any sport. Some will have grown up with older siblings playing so they grow up with the sport which is a definite advantage in understanding how the game is played, and others who have never seen a game played, even on TV and could be an only child. Parents of kids starting out playing the game will also have varying degrees of interest from total lack to total involvement and everything in between which is a major purpose of this book – to help inspire parents to be active with their kids but with good guidance to keep everything in balance. Coaches must always be aware of these starting points and have a degree of flexibility in dealing with everyone involved as your starting points will also develop with every player, every team and every parent you develop a relationship with. Starting points are what I continually look at with my coaching and constantly improving my starting points is something I pride myself on, keeping kids involved in sport for as long as possible and if they develop a lifelong passion for the sport, what a gift they may also pass on as my first coach did for me. A simple philosophy to have is that of advancing your starting points every time you enter the basketball court.

DIFFERENCES IN COACHING BOYS AND GIRLS

When I first started coaching, I gave little thought to the gender I was coaching. I was a young 19-year-old who played elite level junior basketball and thought boys and girls could be treated the same. I had some simple structure and concepts and was a good skills coach insofar as I could demonstrate well and correctly, but most other aspects I can honestly say now I was terrible, especially on individual and team psychology. I only coached for two years then didn't coach again until my late 20's, and still pretty much had the same attitude to both boys and girls. Why treat them any different they're all basketball players?

This all changed late one evening when I was channel surfing our only five commercial TV networks (at the time there was no cable TV) and I came across a documentary called Brain Sex which showed the differences in the male and female brain and the way they process information. This really transformed my coaching mainly when coaching girls and I was no longer under the illusion that they were all just basketball players and I definitely had a new starting point to becoming a better coach with an increased knowledge base.

In simple terms boys respond better to activity and minimal explanation and girls to more detailed explanation and reasons as to why we are doing the activity to achieve certain outcomes. This all has to do with the level of testosterone in the brain and of course there are many kids that fall between the two extremes and I will make adjustments based on this with all the athletes I coach. As we are dealing with beginners in this book, all players will need decent explanations but more importantly reasonable demonstrations to understand how to execute skills, learn concepts and simple plays. As they get older however the real differences between boys and girls really kicks in and being aware will really help the learning process.

Summing Up
Boys – Respond far better to quick explanations, effective demonstrations and productive activity. Keep them moving with purpose and never labour too long in an attempt to make things perfect.

Girls – Respond well to more detailed explanations that state the why for the activity and the outcomes it will provide. Effective demonstrations and productive activity work best and again never labour on any skills or plays to make things perfect.

ROLES OF THE PARENT

Parents have so many roles (books have been written on the subject) and as a parent myself I realise that we all do the best we can within the framework of our domestic, spiritual, financial, social situations and our own childhood experiences. With this in mind I have put together a list of parental Do's and Don'ts that relate to playing basketball and other team sports. Now absolute beginners will be okay but as players and teams gain some experience there will be challenges that do arise.

Parental Do's

1. **Be supportive** – Simple but sometimes overlooked as we parents' get caught up in our busy lives sometimes missing the little things that support our kids. It's not just getting them to games, training and clapping when they do good things on the court. It's also ensuring they're hydrated, that they bring a water bottle to both training and games, they eat a balanced diet, have enough sleep, and it's making sure injuries are treated and managed. After I became an elite junior player one of my parents told me that basketball would do nothing for me and at the time this was devastating as it was my passion in a difficult home situation. Those words still live loud in my mind as a form of motivation for everything I do in the sport.

2. **Be Involved** – This can take many forms and we all have skill sets that can certainly help both our child and their team. Help and encourage your child with learning basic skills, become a team manager and organiser, raise funds for the team if this is needed, look after equipment if the coach and manager don't have the space, be an assistant coach or even the head coach (my first coach had never coached basketball before and was given a book to help him start his coaching career) if there are no options and something everyone can do is be a great cheerleader for the team.

3. **Be on Time** – There is nothing worse for the player and the team when a player turns up late for a game or a training session. Now being late occasionally for training doesn't affect the player and the session too much unless it is the first few and believe me there is a great deal of learning to be done. Being late for games certainly puts a great deal of stress on players and I have seldom seen a player who gets to the game late have even a half decent game, so the lesson is simple – be a little early rather than a little late. If work schedules are a problem, then seek to roster with other parents for trainings and possibly games. Elite coaches certainly penalise players who are late by not letting them play games, but at the beginner level this is certainly not necessary. Being punctual is a great habit to cultivate and a great example for kids.

4. **Set Strong Boundaries** – Boundaries are an interesting subject and from my perspective and experience with thousands of kids and their parents it really is much needed especially in these modern times. Young beginner players will not need the boundaries a teenager would, just a simple set of rules and expected behaviours will suffice. I have had many parents at

my club stop kids playing games, even giving them a few weeks off for neglecting school work, being disrespectful at home, fighting with siblings and similar indiscretions. As coach, I have a quiet word with the player after they have been disciplined and appeal to their sense of being part of a team and making sure in the future that they will be more thoughtful with their behaviour. Banning a player from games hasn't happened a lot at my club, but when it has, I have supported the parents' decision as I know it was a last resort measure and not given for some minor infraction. Once kids understand the boundaries and what is acceptable and not acceptable, they grow as players and as people.

5. **Set Good Examples** – I think we all want the best for our kids and being a positive role model is one of the best ways. Being a good listener, giving guidance, encouragement and having discipline, can take on many forms and one analogy I love is about treating yourself like a multimillion-dollar racehorse, "You would treat it like gold all the best nutrition, the best trainers and equipment". Now I would be the last person to tell or demand how any person should live their life, yet kids need the best possible examples and who better to start a process of positive influence than the people or person who they will spend their formative years with.

Parental Don'ts
Over many years of coaching of what has been a wonderful journey, I have had a very small percentage of negative experiences over many years of coaching of what has been a wonderful journey and so many positive experiences. Most State and regional basketball associations have a Code of Conduct which I recommend all parents read, as it has simple common-sense rules on behaviour.

These are a few things I have encountered that are worth mentioning as they have such a negative effect on the smooth running of the team and everyone's enjoyment.

1. **Supporting Only Your Child and not the Team**
2. **Criticising Other Peoples' Children**
3. **Harass and Undermine the Coach**
4. **Criticise the Referees and opposition Coaches, Players and Parents**
5. **Live your Sporting Failures or Successes Through Your Children**
6. **Drive Kids to the Point of Rebellion, Disinterest and Failure**

With all the above points in the majority of cases, a quiet friendly chat to the person involved by either the coach or another parent helps. Most people I find are very reasonable and I tell them I love their passion for their child but if they could focus this passion on the whole team, it will be far more positive for their own child.

Many of the points in the Do's and Don'ts can be included in some simple rules and guidelines that can be presented to parents when they first join the club or a team. The listed points will certainly give parents and coaches some fuel for thought and possibly curb unproductive behaviour or recognise it as a potential problem that needs to be addressed early for the sake of the kids and team. One of the main reasons I really got involved in this level of basketball was because of a young man who at 15 decided to drop out of basketball and run with a graffiti gang, he tragically died train surfing.

Parents have such a role in the development of their children and Dorothy Law Nolte poem sums it up so wonderfully, this was part of her legacy as a parent educator, practitioner and family counsellor and she taught many people about family dynamics and parenting. She died in 2005, she was 81 and many of you may have grown up with this poem on your refrigerator.

Children Learn What They Live - By Dorothy Law Nolte

If children live with criticism,
They learn to condemn.
If children live with hostility,
They learn to fight.
If children live with ridicule,
They learn to be shy.
If children live with shame,
They learn to feel guilty.
If children live with encouragement,
They learn confidence.
If children live with tolerance,
They learn to be patient.
If children live with praise,
They learn to appreciate.
If children live with acceptance,
They learn to love.
If children live with approval,
They learn to like themselves.
If children live with honesty,
They learn truthfulness.
If children live with security,
They learn to have faith in themselves and others.
If children live with friendliness,
They learn the world is a nice place in which to live.

ROLES OF THE COACH

By now you should have realised that coaching young children will require you to do far more than just learn names, and make substitutions in games. As the coach of a new basketball team you will take on several roles from teacher, cheerleader and the most important role, that of leader of the team. As you become more experienced as a coach there will be far more roles, but the following are the ones you need to adjust to when getting started.

Teacher

You are now in charge of teaching the great game of basketball and with some knowledge will come empowerment and eventually confidence. It is an amazing thing, confidence, in both a player and a coach – too little confidence and you think you can't learn, too much confidence and you think you don't have to learn. I have spent 45 years involved in the game in so many roles and there is still so much I want and can learn. If you are serious about improving any aspect of being a coach or anything in life, then become a student of the game and seek out as much knowledge as you can absorb. In the immortal words of the great martial artist and teacher Bruce Lee.

- **Absorb what is useful**
- **Discard what is useless**
- **Add what is essentially your own**

Being a coach doesn't mean you have to be the fountain of all knowledge on every aspect of basketball, you really only need to be one step ahead of the players and if you maintain this you will always have your players respect. Be honest with your players if you're not sure of something, and then tell them you will find the answer. With a beginner team this will not be a problem, but as you gain more experience as a coach it is something worth remembering.

Positive Cheerleader Coach
In the early weeks of the team training and playing games you will be not only teaching the players the game but also trying to make their experience as positive as possible. It is my personal goal to keep as many players involved in not just the game of basketball but playing sport for the rest of their lives. The key to being a great coach is helping player's correct mistakes they make and then guiding them to do things as well as possible. With a beginner team of young players, you need to be as positive as you possibly can at training but more importantly during the game. Sport is the opposite of school where you get the test first and then the lesson, rather than many lessons then a test. This means your players will not be prepared for what awaits them come game time, they will be tested every time they play the game and will then have to learn the lessons from these tests. There will be some great moments, fun times, bumps and knocks to adjust to, sometimes there will be tears and lucky baskets that make you smile or a heart-breaking close loss. Take it all in your stride and stay positive as there will be another game next week and five minutes after this game most of the kids won't even remember the score or worry about the outcome. You however may think to yourself we dropped so many passes, dribbled too much didn't open the floor up enough on offence and didn't guard to well. All this can be covered at training, so take a few notes and stay positive as you have a new starting point this week.

You Are The Leader
Like it or not, you are the leader of the team and with this comes much responsibility, so far as setting a good example to all around you including most importantly the players under your guidance and the parents who support them. Coach, you will have all these young players looking to you to lead the team, to give them an opportunity to grow as players and people and to learn to work with other players around them within the structure of a team. Many may never have played team sport before and some may have never played catch with anyone. Leadership doesn't sit comfortably with some people but you have no choice, for as a coach it isn't something you can hand over to another unless you no longer want to coach. There will also be an expectation from the parents and guardians of the children under your care and if you have children yourself you will understand that they are the most precious possession they have and must be treated with respect and fairness at all times. This doesn't mean never disciplining them for various things at times when the need arises, as this is what a leader must do.

The 7 Good Traits of a Leader

1. **Confident** – People like and respect a person who has confidence in what they're doing and will follow a leader who possesses this. If this is not you then fake it until you make it, it's okay to act the part until you feel comfortable in this vital role. Remember we want to be confident not cocky or arrogant and the rule here is quite simple: Too little confidence and we will always feel intimidated, unsure, make very few decisions and give very little to the players. Too much confidence and we will feel we know it all and have nothing to learn ourselves.

2. **Respectful** – You have to respect everyone at all times coach even when you don't necessarily agree with people over certain issues. There will come times when a few calls go against you, the players are playing really poorly and it can be frustrating. By giving everyone this simple respect, you will also be held in the same regard as a person that can be trusted.

3. **Example** – This is really important because the players and parents will follow your lead in many respects and whatever is important to you will be important to them. Kids are very impressionable especially the age group you will be dealing with and you get them long before the awkward peer pressured teen aged years. Always be a good example to the players, parents, officials and the opposition teams you face even if they are far stronger and more importantly if you are stronger.

4. **Listen** – Coach, for most of the time you will be the one who talks and imparts your wisdom on all under your guidance, yet sometimes we can get carried away with this and forget the simple courtesy of listening. Part of the example you set is to be a good listener to anyone who is saying something to you, be it child or adult.

5. **Honest and Caring** – Something I pride myself on is telling players and their parents the truth and being honest about where I see the player is at in their current stage of development. Now with the age group you're dealing with this will not be a prime concern of the players but there will be a fair percentage of parents who will question you from time to time. After telling a parent where I feel a player is at as honestly as I can, I will always tell them their child's potential is only limited by their own imagination, the child's not the parent's. You have to care about them as people and as basketball players and seek only to do the best by everyone you're working with.

Remember coach they are not working for you, you are working with them to create great players and teams.

6. **Passion and Enthusiasm** – Coach, it is okay to get a little excited on the side lines and show people that you're enthusiastic and enjoying the game. People love being around passionate and positive upbeat people that enjoy what they're doing. Are you going to feel this way every time you coach a game or run a training session absolutely not, but again you can act it until you really start to feel the part.

7. **Vocal** – Working with this age group really does mean being a vocal as a coach. The system requires that you use **KEY WORDS** a great deal of the time and if the players can hear you it makes a huge difference to their development. Now if your voice is a little on the under developed side then enlist the help of a parent or friend to help get the message across to the players.

Coaching traits to stay away from, are being over-aggressive, bullying, angry, argumentative, nasty and just plain unpleasant to be around. Remember coach you're working with young players who are there to basically have fun, learn some skills and build friendships with their teammates, which for some of them can become lifelong relationships. Two final traits to stay clear of which are polar opposites and I think need to be addressed in some detail are under and over coaching.

• **Under Coaching** – Nothing worse than a coach sitting there saying very little, making very few decisions and generally looking uninterested, as it will not be long until parents start getting frustrated at the team's performance. Training is more or less players messing around, learning very little and lacking anything that resembles a good learning environment. Kids and parents really do deserve better than just a glorified babysitter and if your heart's not in the job it really is better to move on. If it's not the case and you're just a little shy, lacking in confidence and knowledge then the key is education and hopefully you have the foresight to acknowledge this then you can turn things around very quickly especially with beginner kids. A new starting point is certainly possible when armed with the right knowledge and a desire to impart this on the players. This book will certainly be a great tool and you can also seek out a mentor to give you some feedback and even a little help with the team from time to time.

- **Over Coaching** – This is a trap many new coaches can fall into as they try to help the team by giving way too many instructions and basically telling every single player what they need to be doing on every single play. This type of coach thinks the game is all about them and not the players, which is a huge mistake. The players are on their own journeys and although we want to help them as much as possible and speed up the process, we must still allow them the opportunity to make mistakes (of which there will be plenty regardless of what you do or say), develop and learn as they train and play games. Now this book is designed to help speed up their development but you still have to give them a little space to discover the answers to the many tests they will get while playing the game. Give them knowledge, guide and develop their skills, let them make their mistakes and then help them discover the answers with some correction and a little hard work during training, and feedback in games. The **KEY WORDS** system in this book will certainly give you the tools to avoid over coaching.

Coaching Styles

There are so many coaching styles from loud and aggressive personalities to quiet, relaxed, rather sedate and easy going, that have all won major titles at one time or another. What works for one coach will not necessarily work for you and coaches we are not in the business of winning major titles, but creating great players, great teams and great kids who have a love of staying healthy and will keep playing sport. My best advice is to just be you (to thine own self be true) and educate yourself and coach as much as possible to gain experience and expertise. A deep respect will come from the team or squad when they put their trust in you that you can help them become better basketball players and people.

GETTING STARTED

"Where do I start?" I guess everyone has faced this at some point in their life especially when taking on a new challenge. Once the motivation has been established to take on the task of coaching young basketball players, then the next step is a little planning and some follow through on the following points.

1. Set Some Simple Written Goals – It is a sad reality that the majority of people set no written Goals. For a beginner basketball team, it is wise to have progressive Goals and benchmarks over several time periods. This book outlines the way to structure training, teach skills, plenty of drills and training plans along with coaching games. It would be wise as a new coach to write simple plans and a few notes on players and their progress.

2. Become a Student of the Game – To become really good at anything you really need to develop the skills to become successful and with basketball there is so much to learn. You will certainly be learning the game from this book and gaining experience by just running training sessions and game coaching. Once you are past this beginner stage there is such a wealth of knowledge for coaches with far more advanced basketball options on every conceivable aspect of coaching. You can read more books, watch DVD's and attend clinics by experienced coaches as a great way to increase your knowledge. Now you will never use everything you learn but you will learn better ways to teach advanced skills, different ways to teach the same skills that keep them fresh for players, modified ways to improve your teams and save time and great ways to communicate from master coaches. With all the games and training sessions I have conducted I am still learning and honing my skills as I owe this to every athlete I work with. I hope all coaches become students of the game by talking to other coaches, joining forums and websites on coaching and also do some research outside of just basketball coaching on psychology, strength and conditioning training for the age level you're working with.

3. Use a Simple Plan – There are training plans and tips on game coaching in later chapters which I feel are a great asset to an inexperienced coach and the old adage of failing to plan is planning to fail comes to mind. With beginners, having a training plan will keep things moving just in case you get bogged down trying to perfect something and sacrifice other segments that must be taught. Even if you don't use the training plans from this book which I highly recommend, have some notes on what you will cover and it's always best to keep it simple.

4. The Better You Teach the More They Will Want to Learn – My first basketball coach Mike Baker was an interesting man for so many reasons. He was my biggest inspiration to become a coach and I always thought if I could be half as good as him, I would be an excellent coach. He was an ex-army drill sergeant in the British Armed Forces and was a Physical Education Teacher by profession but had never coached basketball until a group of students presented him with a book and asked him to coach them. He had a big barrel chest and a voice that could be heard two suburbs away so he was certainly an imposing presence at training and in games. Mike was an interesting personality hard, tough as nails and he did put the fear of God into you as a player but he was the fairest coach I have ever had. When

you heard your first name in a sentence, feel good things were coming your way but if it was your surname then usually a harsh example or correction was to follow. Mike taught me more in my nine months with him than all the coaches I had in the next ten years and some of these coaches were State and National coaches. The thing about a great teacher is not only do you learn, but your motivation and desire to learn more increases also. Even though most of us feared Mike initially we were there at every training session keen, ready and loving learning the game. One of his original players went on to captain our Olympic team, Mike was such an inspiration to so many of his players who not only learnt how to play but were eager to learn more.

5. Have Fun and Enjoy the Journey – Life throws up many challenges along the way, good times, bad times are all lessons and experiences we all have and my advice to coaches, is to have fun and enjoy the journey. Yes, it will be hard work at times but working with young kids and giving them the valuable life skills that team sport brings is so rewarding. It is great meeting the young adults I coached as kids, as they always have many stories to share that I may have forgotten on past triumphs and failures. It's also great to catch up and see what they have done and are currently doing with their lives. My goals at our club are not just to produce good players and great teams but great people who will be respectful and eventually contribute to their communities and hopefully give back to the sport as players, coaches, fans and even parents themselves one day.

EQUIPMENT

Although there is so much advanced equipment to help every aspect of skill development, beginners will really only need the basic equipment to play the game.

- **Basketball Shoes** – Players should wear properly fitting basketball shoes as comfort here is far more important than looks and style. Having suffered through many blisters as a young player myself this is vital. There is an incredible range of basketball shoes in the market place with so many styles and names that it is often difficult to know which shoe to buy. I recommend that you select shoes that are within your price range and with so many factory outlets and online shops you can always find a suitable shoe. The shoes should have good ankle support to prevent rolled or sprained ankles, as running shoes have very little to help a basketball player with the lateral movement they will use during a game. The shoes need good grip to allow players to make quick stops and starts on the basketball court. I recommend high cut basketball shoes which give the ankles far better support. A small hint for parents when breaking in a new pair of shoes is to place band aids around the small toes and back of the foot where the shoes may rub. Players should also wear them around for a day or two to prevent major blisters the first few times in games.

- **Basketball Socks** – Socks also come in many different shapes and sizes from anklet styles to old-school knee-high tubes. It's really important that the sock fits well and wicks away sweat from the feet. If you're wearing one pair of socks make sure they're reasonably thick, many recommend players wear two pairs of athletic socks to help prevent toes and feet from blistering, which will also provide a little more comfort under foot. Comfort is important here both pre, during and post-game.

- **Basketball Shorts** – Should be loose-fitting but comfortable so that they allow freedom of movement and should definitely have no pockets which can injure thumbs. The shorts need to allow freedom of movement without any restrictions to the lower body.

- **Basketball Shirt or Jersey** – A comfortable basketball singlet, tank-top or loose-fitting t-shirt that wicks sweat away from the body should be worn which allows players freedom of movement without having their arms or upper body restricted.

- **Knee Pads** – I recommend that players wear knee pads especially if they like to dive on the floor after the ball as these will help keep the skin on the knees and not on the court.

- **Mouth Guard** – This is a parents' choice but I recommend that players should wear a mouth guard to protect their teeth, tongue, lips and cheeks from injuries caused by accidental contact. More and more players are wearing mouth guards these days due to the close contact during a game or training, especially near the basket. Some parents prefer to wait until kids lose their baby teeth but I feel players should protect their mouths from injury.

- **Basketballs** – Every player should have their own basketball that they can bring to training or use to train with in their own time. This will certainly help them improve their skills and they should use a ball that is the right size for their age specific group. The main key when selecting a basketball is the surface, you're using it on. A good leather ball will be damaged when bounced on outdoor courts which suit the cheaper rubber ball. These days balls come in many different materials that are suited for both inside and outside, so this is only limited by your budget.

- **Basketball Rings** – This isn't necessarily basketball player equipment but eventually it is something that will certainly help players develop their shooting and overall game. Rings and backboards come in many different shapes and sizes from free standing to ones you can bolt onto a garage or brick wall. It will be dependent on the amount of space and area you have, however so many schools have basketball rings these days that players can use. As with most products you will only be limited by budget and there are free standing options, along with inground and bolt rings and backboards that attach to garages.

Check out the resources pages in the back of the book for retailers that supply all of the above.

CHAPTER 2
Essential Offensive Fundamentals

CHAPTER 2
ESSENTIAL OFFENSIVE FUNDAMENTALS

The biggest impact a parent can make on a young beginner basketball player will be in assisting their child to develop their basic offensive skills. A coach and the team will for most parts have limited time together so skill development could be slow as the overall focus will be on all the team members and it is here the parent can get involved beyond just encouraging their child. The coach and the parents working together to help the young athlete can be such a great partnership and can only benefit players and team. It is vital to have a checklist of the essential basic skills players will need to have to not only help their development, but that of the team. It is also a good opportunity to teach basic rules of the game while instructing the players in line with the skills they are learning.

OFFENSIVE SKILLS CHECKLIST

- **Footwork – Leading – Cutting**
- **Triple Threat – Pivoting – Catching – Passing**
- **Dribbling**
- **Shooting**
- **Rebounding**
- **Fakes**

This list breaks down the skills you will be teaching so make sure you grasp and understand that these basics are the true building blocks of the game of basketball.

FOOTWORK

Footwork is where I begin every training session I have ever conducted with new players and teams. I also explain to them that even if the ball was shared equally among only ten players for both teams involved in a game over 40 minutes, each player would only have the ball for a total of four minutes which is simple math that most players understand. The other side to the equation is that they don't have the ball for the other 36 minutes or 90% of the time is spent without the ball so you could spend it standing around which is what some players will do or you can impress on your young players the value of becoming really good with their feet and also their eyes and brains teaching them to think and move without the ball in their hands.

V - Cut (Zigzag)

The V Cut is the first piece of footwork I teach to new players which is quite simple and a very important part of player's offensive game. The ability to move side to side or laterally cannot be emphasised enough as on court there will be a defensive player directly in front of them that they have to break free of or get past. Have your players line up on the baseline and then run a few steps on a 45-degree angle towards the sideline. If they are heading to the right have them stop with their right foot forward and shift most of their weight to this foot and then push off in the opposite direction to the left again for a few steps. Repeat this process all the way down the floor in a zigzag pattern until they reach the opposite baseline. I tell the players I want to hear their sneakers squeaking as they head up and down the court. Have your players start slowly until they find their feet so to speak and then speed up with the emphasis on sharp changes in direction side to side, not running by circling which is not as sharp and takes longer to change direction.

Hesitation Lead (SLOW ZIG – FAST ZAG)

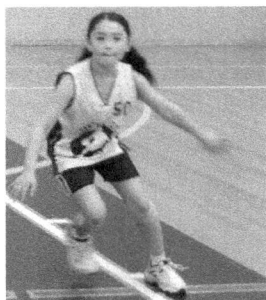

This is the getting open for the ball and scoring lead all players will absolutely love once they master it as they will always be open for the ball and this allows them to get more shots which is very motivating. Understand though players all develop at their own pace and some will take time to develop this vital component as many will feel that standing still and screaming their teammates names hundreds of times a game is the best way. This must be constantly drilled and is

easily taught with the key words **SLOW ZIG – FAST ZIG**. Taking a few slow steps or even one slow step either left or right (**SLOW ZIG**) then pushing off hard in the opposite direction (**FAST ZAG**) with a target hand up so their teammate can direct the ball in the right position away from the defence and in front of their teammates lead. You can use this as a warm up without the ball after running the V-Cut drill but I find it is far more effective when used in conjunction with the basketball. I also get players to draw it in the air with both their hands to further plant the seeds of what they will do in the future, sooner rather than later.

Contact lead

Basketball is a contact sport no doubt about it and as contact is part of the game I try and introduce this as soon as possible into our training sessions. Now it would be great if we were all born with superhuman speed and the ability to avoid any and all contact during the game but regardless how quick a player is, they will eventually run into other players mostly from the other team. Building on the hesitation lead we can use this to our advantage and utilise contact as an essential part of the game to gain an advantage so far as better position and actually getting open for the pass. In this lead the offensive player seeks initial contact with their opponent by moving their body into them via hip and leg contact rather than upper body where cheap fouls will be given if the contact is pushing off with hands and arms. Once contact is established the offensive player seeks to cut the defence out by placing their leg across the defenders' body blocking them out from the direction they intend to lead to get open for the ball. Once the offensive player cuts the defence out of the direction they intend on getting open for the ball they gently nudge the defence with their hip trying to rock them back on their heels giving the offence an even greater advantage once they lead usually several steps. If the defence is applying heavy pressure this is the best way to counter this by creating the contact and leading off the opponent, rather than trying to out manoeuvre them with foot speed alone. It is important that the player leading get eye

contact with the passer otherwise it will be a wasted effort as they will not get the ball even if they get wide open.

Final Thoughts
"**The better the footwork the better the player**" is a little saying I use at training constantly and get players to repeat often, planting the seeds of greatness into each individual so that they may enjoy the game with a greater feeling of freedom. Players who stand flat-footed, rooted to the ground like a tree, will get frustrated and will probably quit, never really giving basketball or any other sport much of a chance. Movement is essential for the greater enjoyment of the game, not to mention the scoring opportunities it will create. Time spent on footwork is never wasted and once a young player gets the concepts and actions of the various leads, their longevity in the game will be guaranteed even if they are not great shooters, they will be able to get the ball moving with safe leads and be a trusted member of the team.

JUMP AND STRIDE STOP - PIVOTING - TRIPLE THREAT - CATCHING - PASSING

Jump Stop
The jump stop is the first of the two stopping techniques I teach and something that should not take a long time to learn. For some players with coordination problems it may take some time to master, yet with persistent practice should pick up without too much trouble. As the name suggests players jump to stop, landing equally on both feet staying in balance and ready to play. I prefer players make short sharp jump stops as opposed to more long jump styles which will make keeping balance at speed quite difficult. You can use this technique in conjunction with footwork drills have them jump stop then continue several times up and down the floor or on the coach's whistle. You will definitely use this during passing and dribbling drills.

Stride Stop

The Stride Stop will be the stopping action used the majority of the time and will be an important teaching point when it comes to shooting the set shot. The Stride Stop is in simple terms planting one-foot down stationary on the floor before the other foot. I call the first foot down the anchor and ideally if you're right-handed this should be your left foot, and if you're left-handed your right foot down first, as it will help keep you in good balance to protect the ball but more importantly shoot the ball. This also helps a player stop when running at high speed and will become important when learning how to pivot. This is a great time to explain the travel rule to players when you finally introduce basketballs to the drill or at home playing in the backyard.

PIVOTING

Having taught the concept of the anchor foot on the Stride Stop we can now apply this to pivoting. It really does amaze me the number of players who have played for many years that find this skill so hard to do or maintain, they move the ball from side to side with a pressuring defender and either lose it or end up having a jump ball. Teaching pivoting is easier once the players understand the concept of keeping their anchor foot on the floor. I tell the players to lift up their heel off the floor and imagine they have a long nail through their shoe down through the ball of their foot and all they can do is turn in a circle. Initially we work on taking three small jab steps to complete a full circle both forwards and backwards. We practice this at first without the ball, then with the ball, then under pressure in a three-stage process easing players through the stages so they eventually get comfortable with the skill.

TRIPLE THREAT

The legendary coach Hubie Brown calls this the looking good position and I have to agree with the description of the triple threat. Basically, whenever a player catches the ball within shooting range, they should face the basket in a lowered position and for right-handed shooters have their right foot slightly forward. The ball is held at the midpoint of the body and from this position the player has 3 forms of attacking the defensive player.

Shoot, Dribble and Pass
This gives the stance its name triple threat and yet I feel it has far more options in that a player can fake a shot, dribble and pass before making one of the three moves. It will take some time before most players really get the hang of the triple threat, but as they gain experience and confidence, they will use it and will become one of many weapons that can create scoring opportunities for themselves and their teammates.

CATCHING

Catching is always the first skill I teach before passing and if you ignore this then I would expect a few tears at the first few training sessions as a basketball can hurt a great deal when you get hit in the face, or in the lower region of the trunk. I never really thought much about teaching catching, thinking that all kids could catch something as big as a basketball, until I saw a legend of the game Pistol Pete Maravich teaching it on one of his basic videos. I now use the shooting hand slightly over and the off-hand slightly under technique as a standard in our program and with beginners teach this as soon as we get into ball work. It has cut the rate of players getting hit in the face dramatically and before we do any passing drills. It also places all players in a ready to shoot position, which rapidly speeds up this process teaching players to be a quicker decision maker close to the basket.

Most kids when they first start to catch a ball or other objects as a toddler will place both hands out, palms up, and grab at what is being thrown to them. Some will hold it forward and grasp it in their hands others will pull it into their chest to secure the item. Now this habit may follow them right up to the time they step on a basketball court and start playing so be prepared for the hits in the face if you don't teach them the hand slightly over, hand slightly under technique straight off. Believe me having suffered through many a players' tears; they can then develop a very real fear of the ball as they close their eyes, backing up, travelling constantly and worry that the ball actually coming their way will hurt them. Having been hit in the face by a basketball I can tell you it hurts like hell and brings even the toughest of players to tears when hit on the nose so the quicker players use hand over hand under technique, the safer they will be. As a young coach working with players with some experience catching wasn't a big problem. It wasn't until I started with beginners that the importance of technique was a major concern. I will never let absolute beginners start any passing drill without teaching the hand over under catching technique.

Points of Emphasis for Pre-and Post-Catch

- Have knees slightly bent and maintain your balance whether standing or moving

- Keep your eye on the ball until the catch is made also called seeing the ball into the hands

- Once the ball is caught, eyes up and look towards your basket. This is a great habit as players will become better decision makers as they are seeing the court, the defence and the position of teammates.

- Look after the ball and take either a protection or a triple threat stance

- Make good decisions

Simple Reasons for Dropping the Ball

- Not ready for the ball

- Not balanced to make the catch

- Taking the eyes off the ball

- Thinking of what they're going to do and not concentrating on catching the ball first

- Distracted by surroundings, noise and physical pressure from defenders

I have added the reasons players drop the ball to emphasise the importance of concentrating and being ready to play as they owe this to themselves and their teammates. Coaches keep an eye on your training sessions and make sure dropped passes are not a key component otherwise you will have miserable games and a lack of possessions to actually get shots ups. When players have the catching technique down, they can then move onto other important skills ie simply stopping with the ball, as every player needs to either jump stop or stride stop and will use both as they develop their game to higher levels of skill.

PASSING

Passing is one of the most under-utilised skills in the game today as many dominant players want to dribble rather than pass. Passing is one of the backbones of building a team and bringing players of various levels of skill into a working unit. The basic passes needed are listed below in the order we teach them and even though most coaches teach the two-handed chest pass first up, many beginners will pass with only their dominant hand to begin with and eventually with some training will develop the use of both hands.

With all passing it is really important that players understand that they need to use their entire body and use their power base with most skills used in basketball. When teaching the two-handed passes, I liken the action of pushing down a wall and ask the players "If I was to push down a wall how would I do it? Would I use one hand to push the wall down or even both arms pushing out standing still, without using my feet?" After these questions are posed to the players, I then have them show me how they would push the wall down and usually all the players step into the pushing of the imaginary wall down and it is from here we have now established the power base by which we look to execute all our passes. Using the pivot foot as the anchor and the lead foot to push forward to the target, we now have the technique to generate power in the pass.

Chest Pass – Holding the ball at chest level, securely in both hands with fingers spread and thumbs on top of the ball, keeping elbows in towards the hips, step forward with the lead foot towards the target and snap the wrists on release of the ball putting backspin on the pass with the thumbs ending down. The back spin keeps the ball in the air longer and always encourage strong, crisp passing as opposed to soft loopy lob passes which anyone including the opposition can catch.

The two handed chest pass focus and follow through to the target.

Bounce Pass – The starting position is the same as the chest pass and the actual mechanics of the pass is identical but you're passing the ball off the floor and keeping this in mind the ball must be passed harder as it loses speed on contact with the court. The pass must be aimed two thirds of the way to the target with good back spin to make it sit up for the easy catch. One of my old coaches reminded me frequently that the bounce pass is a scoring pass and I encourage players to use it in that situation, I also encourage smaller players playing against larger defenders to use it as much as possible.

Overhead Pass – This time the set-up is above the head just forward of the ears with even pressure on the ball with both hands and fingers spread and thumbs pointing down and elbows slightly forward in a reverse set-up to the chest pass. As with the previous passes using the anchor foot to push off and the lead foot to generate the power step towards the target, keeping the ball held at the starting point and not allowing it to creep to the back of the head, snap the wrists and launch the ball strong towards your teammate. Beginners will most of the time only use this pass in the game while under pressure.

One – Handed Push Pass – This will be the pass most beginner players will use as most players will be one hand dominant before they start playing basketball and parents and coaches please note, over the course of time everyone can be trained to use both sides of their body. Starting position is at the chest and this time the player steps forward into the pass but is only using one hand with the opposite hand on the side of the ball pushing out towards the target and snapping the wrist on the follow through to the target. It is vital that practice is spent on both sides of the body as this type of pass works really well under pressure which leads into the next element of adding pass fakes.

Baseball Pass – Eventually players will want to throw passes further down the court and it is a pass I introduce to younger players after they have a good handle on controlling the ball with both hands. Older beginners however should be strong enough in most cases to use it at training and then games. The technique requires attention to detail as the anchor foot this time is the same as the passing hand which is opposite to shooting and some of the other passes. For a right-handed pass the ball is held in both hands and brought up to the right ear as the left foot is raised off the floor. The right hand moves behind the ball and is then directed towards the target as is the left foot driving toward the floor as the ball is released with a snap of the wrist and the opposite hand points to the intended receiver. I prefer that the players keep the pass compact and under control.

Pass Fakes – A really great weapon for a young player to develop as soon as possible that will be a great asset when players find themselves under pressure with the ball which in a beginner game, will be pretty much most of the time until the values of **SPLIT**, spacing and body contact leads are developed. Faking is a great way to move the defensive player and create space for easier passes to teammates. The following are some simple pass fake / pass make options that all players should adopt as part of a plan to counter an opponent. The opponents' size will also be a factor.

Fake and Pass Options

- Fake High /Pass Low

- Fake Low Pass High

- Fake Left Pass Right

- Fake Right Pass Left

When teaching faking the emphasis here is on selling the fake (making it realistic enough so the defence will react to it) and the key here is to only move the ball at medium speed move to the halfway point of the fake then quickly making the pass in the opposite direction. If the fake is too fast the defender will not react and if it is too slow, they may slap the ball away or steal it. Pass faking is a great way to create easier passes and scoring opportunities, teach it, reteach it and keep emphasising its importance and it will help young beginner players enjoy the game more and reduce mistakes.

Final Thoughts
As a coach I praise the passer far more than I ever do the scorer which sends a message to the players that passing is important to me and eventually this will also be showing itself in the games. Some of my favourite key words are **NEXT PASS** and **GIVE IT** to promote this in the game, and I love it when I can call out **"GREAT TEAMWORK"** after some great passing creates an easy score.

DRIBBLING

Keep it really simple here parents and coach in that with beginner players they do not need every different type of dribble that currently exists. It is good to keep all the players facing towards the front and not turning their backs on the play to encourage better habits and teamwork.

Technique – A player starts in a comfortable stance with knees slightly bent for balance, then I have a player form a finger spread suction cup with the hands and we work on wrist snap and simulate dribbling below the elbow, before we actually use the ball. Once players start using the ball I have them stand still and dribble, while working on ball control with the finger tips and pads (real tiny hands just get these on the ball) keeping the head and eyes up. Make players practice stationery dribbling on both hands before moving to control dribble advancing the ball up the court.

Control – A control dribble is keeping the ball below the level of the elbow and bouncing strong and in rhythm with the feet usually bouncing on the right hand in step with the left foot and the left hand in step with the right foot. The focus here is advancing the ball under control with eyes up and equal time is given to both hands and I would encourage players to work two to three times longer on their off-hand to help balance dribbling strength on both sides of the body. Balance is really important here and a strong emphasis on keeping head and eyes up.

Protection – As the word protection would suggest this dribble is designed to be kept out of harm's way not allowing the defence an easy steal. It is here players learn to position their bodies between their opponents and the ball with a protection arm up and angling their bodies to either side to protect the ball. This can be done in a stationary and moving position and comes back to one of the first rules of basketball I ask players to "**LOOK AFTER THE BALL**" and the protection dribble really goes a long way to achieve this. Make sure players hold the protection up at all times but do not push their opponents away with it otherwise they can receive an offensive foul. I like players to make a fist as it keeps the protection arm stronger than a limp hand. The ball is behind the head so this dribble really encourages the good habit of eyes up and forward scanning the court. For better control keep the ball below the elbow and bounce it strong.

Speed – Most players will become very good at the control dribble and develop a really nice rhythm with the ball however if they use this on the speed dribble it will not maximise their natural speed. The technique here is to dribble the ball at chest height, pushing it out forward under reasonable control taking 3+ steps for every bounce. Important to note that the ball should be at chest height and not too low or too high as well as all the basic fundamentals of dribbling keeping head and eyes up and maintaining balance applies.

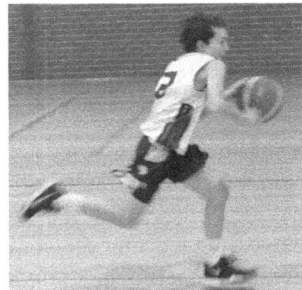

Crossover – After you have the basic control and speed dribble in motion, we now start to introduce basketball moves designed to get past opponents and create passing and scoring opportunities. The crossover can be performed in a straight line or veering right or left and for practice purposes can be done in a zigzag pattern with and without defence. The crossover is a sharp change of direction from one hand to the other and can be easily performed from both control and speed dribble. From a control dribble the ball needs to be lowered to knee high and pushed across the front of the body with a sharp snap of the wrist as the lower the ball the harder it is for opponents to steal or bat it away, this works really well in a zigzag pattern. When moving in a straight line I like the ball to be wide of the body to shift the defence wider and across to create a better angle to get by an opponent. There must be a heavy emphasis here on snapping the ball low and sharp and encourage young players to make it part of their skill set sooner rather than later.

Hesitation (Stop and Go) – This is a great dribble move that really is seldom used in games at many levels yet it is so effective, so it's really hard to understand why. The hesitation or stop and go dribble is easy to teach and learn but it does require some attention to detail from both player and coach. The hesitation dribble can be used with other types of dribbling and the basic technique is to come to a sudden stop, lower the body slightly, bouncing the ball below the elbow for several bounces before taking a big first step, pushing off strong and putting distance between themselves and the opposition player. To help beginner players understand the concept I tell them it's like having a running race and getting to say go. Not only do you get to say go but you can in most cases also choose the direction, which makes it even harder for defence to predict both

start and direction. This is a great dribble to create scoring opportunities and I often tell young players the story of Jack who scored 15 points a game from a hesitation dribble and a left-hand layup. He is now a senior elite player and was already carving up defences with his signature move at the tender age of seven. He still uses it to great effect and makes it hard for defenders to guard him as he stops suddenly, then explodes past them on his way to either create his own shot or assist a teammate. Spend a little time on this one coaches and parents, it will certainly help turn young players into better ball handlers and make them very hard to defend.

Retreat – This is a great get out of trouble dribble which still keeps the player facing to the front and seeing teammates and defence. It amazes me that even experienced players will dribble forward then stop sometimes in the key and be swarmed by pressuring defenders with absolutely no passing options to get out of trouble, which usually ends up with your team losing the ball on a turnover. It starts from the protection position backing up quickly which will give a player a few seconds to seek out a teammate for an easy pass under less pressure or cut back towards the centre of the court. It works even better if you fake a hard step forward then retreat.

Spin – This is a dribble that I usually wait before I teach really young beginners, as I much prefer they face up the court and particularly the basket when they are in control of the ball. The spin dribble by its very nature means the player has to turn their back on their opponents and also their teammates, so when teaching this you must always emphasise protecting the ball as a key to executing the dribble. Start in a control dribble on a 45degree angle which makes it easier for the player just learning the dribble. As they move forward dribbling with their right hand, have them plant their left foot forward off their right and then pivot backwards, swinging their right foot and pulling the ball behind on the spin with the same hand, keeping it protected with the body. It is really important that the player turns their head quickly while making the move so they can see the court and bounce the ball on their left hand in the opposite 45degree angle, again protecting it with their body. While dribbling forward on the left hand, have the player plant their right foot and spin backwards to their right side repeating this process as the player makes their way down the court. The biggest mistake players will make is to not pull the ball backwards with the same hand but do this with the opposite hand which can give a defender an opportunity to steal the ball. This can also slow the spin move down and can cause a player to carry the ball by swinging instead of snapping the ball backwards. To counter this, you can basically force a player to use only one hand and spin in a square pattern, so they can only use one hand practicing the same move over and over again. This really helps the player master the move and I combine this into a 3 dribble move and various shots at the basket, utilising the edge of the key and the elbows at both ends of the free throw line.

This is an advanced dribble and to help the players pick up the concept of both pulling back with the same hand along with protecting and actually finding their balance and rhythm with the dribble, use the following drill. Set-up cones in a square and in the diagrams here we use the key to map out a path for players to follow. This simple drill can be done individually or in a team and is a great way to teach the spin dribble as it only allows one hand to do all the dribbling building on correct technique. Players dribble anti-clockwise only on their right hand spinning backwards as they reach the first cone and spin backwards pulling the ball back towards the next cone and only allowing the right hand to bounce the ball, keeping the left hand out of the drill until the very end where the player can shoot the ball and then they can touch the ball with the left hand to support the shot. I use this drill to teach the main components of the dribble and we spend as much time if not a little more on the opposite side of the body to balance the practice and give the players confidence on both sides of the body. You can shorten the distance of the square or widen it to have the players work at speed and the choice of shots and moves are only limited by your imagination. I usually put the shot in just to break up the drill so the players don't end up becoming dizzy through constant spins and you can also set-up four cones rather than the three in the diagrams and have the players change direction on blowing the whistle so they get some reaction work also. With beginners however, it is more important that good technique is not compromised by pure speed until the player masters the move.

Conclusion
Dribbling is a very simple component of offence as the floor is flat the ball is round and when the ball hits the floor it will bounce back up. Kids can gain great confidence as ball handlers providing they put a decent amount of work into developing their skills. It can take some time to develop into a great shooter, but dribbling needs no ring, just a ball and a reasonably flat surface, and a little hard work and dedication.

Keys Points to Dribbling

• Make a suction cup with the hand and spread the fingers

• Snap the wrist and dribble strong

• Keeps the eyes up when dribbling

• Use both hands equally or practice more on the off-hand

• Practice all the basic dribbles and encourage the use of them in a game

• The pass is still the best way to move the ball quickly down the court

SHOOTING

This is easily the most enjoyable part of the game of basketball. Shooting hoops is very important to the development of the team and it will be the part that most players will love doing. Scoring baskets always brings a smile to the face and kids will practice this part of the game for many hours and will certainly celebrate it during games. There are many shots a player will need to develop as they progress in their basketball careers, but you only need to worry about three types of shots.

Set Shot – A shot where the players' feet are set and they then shoot the ball. This shot will be shot under the eyes.
- **Overhead Shot** – A little more advanced than the set shot and especially effective for taller players close to the basket and shot above the eyes.
- **Layup** – A running shot where the player shoots the ball without stopping in a fluid movement.
- **Set shot off the catch and dribble** – This will be important to practice as most players will use this until they master the layup. It will also be used in conjunction with various fakes as the players progress and develop as shooters.

Basic Set Shot
This is the first shot that you will teach and it is important to start with good technique right away. I like to use a simple technique with three **KEY WORDS ROLL, UP and SNAP.** Just before I teach the three **KEY WORDS,** I get all players to work on their footwork and placement and then teach them where their power base is. I have every player stand on the three-point line facing the basket and the coach stands just behind the free throw line to keep all the players within their vision.

Footwork – I get every player to stand with their feet together and explain that this is a really poor position so far as their balance is concerned, and to demonstrate this I have one player come out the front and get them to face the group standing straight up with their feet together. I then stand behind the player holding up one finger and then I press this one finger against the players shoulder and gently push them off balance so all the players start to understand that feet together is a really poor starting position when shooting the ball. From here with the understanding of what poor balance is, we move on to holding up the hand they will shoot the ball with then we move the opposite foot halfway back to their other foot and then open up the foot to have both feet in line with the shoulders. This may be slightly wider or narrower which is quite okay so long as they feel comfortable with their knees slightly bent forward over the toes keeping the head up with a nice straight trunk. If the player is right-handed, they should point their right foot directly at the basket and the left foot can be either pointed in that direction or slightly pointing outwards so long as they are comfortable.

Powerbase – Once the players are in a comfortable set-up position for the shot I have them pair up so they can realise where the power for the shot comes from. I have one teammate stand behind the other and press their hands down on their shoulders as firmly as they can. From this position, I get the player who is being held down to bend their knees a little further and then push-up against the pressure several times making sure they get up on their toes and keep their body nice and straight as they lift up. Make sure you match up players here of a similar size and then have them take turns holding their hands on each other's shoulders and really feel where the power is coming from to shoot the ball. For safety reasons make sure the players push straight up and not throw their heads back and accidentally hit their teammates. They also must push-up from their shooting stance, not feet together or parallel. From the power base we head into the three **KEY WORDS** for shooting **ROLL – UP – SNAP**.

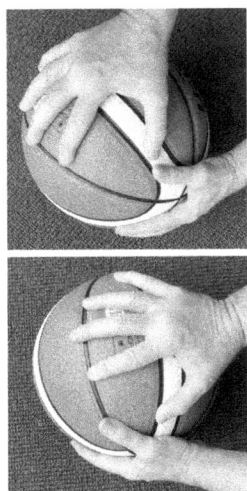

ROLL – I believe a shooter should shoot with a slight rolling action as this will develop with time into an overhead shot and eventually a jump shot. Now with young players of limited strength who are just learning, the most important thing is to develop a simple compact technique using the lower and upper body working together to create a nice fluid action. The ball starts just under the chin with the shooting hand behind the ball and the opposite hand on the side with the thumbs forming either an L or a T

joint. The shooting elbow starts on the side of the body and is in a relaxed natural position. I don't like the elbow starting directly under the ball as it will usually end up with a player putting side spin on the ball after they release the ball from the hand. From this starting point the player now rolls the ball gently forward bending the knees forward over the toes keeping the head and trunk still, moving only the arms and the legs.

UP – From the roll with the knees forward of the toes the player now pushes up with their legs bringing the elbow under the ball while keeping the back straight up to the release point and the **SNAP**. It is important that the elbow and the hand form a straight line (also referred to as a straight one) up to the release of the ball, as there is a saying in basketball that "where the elbow goes the hand is sure to follow". Make sure the upper and lower body are working together and not fighting each other with stop actions during the up phase of the shot.

SNAP – The snap is just my simple word for follow through as many coaches ask their players to snap their wrists on release of the ball. This snap of the wrist will place back spin on the ball provided the player has kept their hand parallel to the floor at the **SNAP**. I always want players to shoot with a medium arc on the ball and a reasonable amount of back spin to give the shot a little softness. I explain to players that the ring is a flat target and in order to make a basket you need to shoot up and on top of this flat target. Shooting at the flat target will only bring frustrating misses as the ball rebounds off the ring and seldom goes in. I ask all players to make sure they shoot up to the ring and use another little saying quite regularly that "if it's not up, it's not in".

Simple Target

There are only two targets when shooting the basketball, the ring and the backboard. The backboard should always be used when a player is close to the basket and on the ideal 45-degree angle between the ring and the backboard as this is the most efficient way to score. Players should always use the backboard on and between the 45-degree angles when within a meter of the ring. As players move further from the ring and also shooting along the baseline the second target now comes into play. I explain to the players that the ring is a flat target (it certainly is round and large but it does sit flat) and in order to make a basket you need to shoot up and on top of the flat target. Shooting straight at the flat target will only bring frustrating misses as the ball rebounds off the ring and only a lucky bounce will result in a basket. I instruct all players to shoot

the ball up to the ring and use a little saying quite regularly "if it's not up it's not in". Once players understand the concept of shooting the ball up to the target I then focus on their eyes and give them a specific target to shoot at, one that is guaranteed to put the ball in the basket. Some coaches like players to aim at the back of the ring and shoot slightly short and others prefer to aim at the front of the ring and shoot slightly longer. I personally don't like either of these options preferring to focus on a far more specific target - the **W** that holds the net to the ring. Now when the ball actually hits this target it will be inside the ring, it cannot be anywhere else. There are twelve **W's** attached to the ring holding the net on for most rings and there will always be one in a player's line of sight. This will certainly increase shots made once it becomes a habit for the shooter to focus on this simple but effective target. Not all rings have the **W's** clearly visible (some may be taped or looped over another ring) yet focusing on the back of the net just under the ring will bring very positive results with good technique and a decent amount of practice. A size six basketball can fit almost two and a half times into the ring so there is plenty of room for error and still score a basket. To prove to players just how big the ring is, have them lay on the floor directly under the basket and then shoot the ball into the basket so they can see this for themselves. It actually looks like an orange passing through the net from this vantage point.

Time is never wasted on emphasising good shooting technique, along with sighting a specific target and with new players it never has to be too technical. I like the simple **KEY WORD** concept of **ROLL UP SNAP** for shooting, as the words are a reflection of the action required and will be a good starting point for brand new players. Make sure they get the legs involved in the shot as early as possible, so they will not get too discouraged when shooting free throws.

Layups

The layup is the running shot that all players should learn as soon as possible and I start to teach this from the second or third training session. What appears on the outside to be the simplest of shots, will take some of your players quite a while to learn the basic footwork and then coordinate this with their upper body to produce a fluid and flowing shot. A coach and player will need some patience and persistence with this process but once mastered it will be a skill they will have for as long as they keep playing the game. Like the basic set shot the layup has a step by step process of teaching that players must progress through in order to learn the shot. Some of the players will pick up the skill quite quickly and others will take some time which is okay as kids develop in their own time, but you can certainly speed up this progress in rapid time. Like all other skills you will teach, there are steps to take to eventually create a successful result. Have all your players line up facing the wall with a ball each about two steps back and have them place the ball behind them on the floor. I always have the players learn the components of the layup facing the wall first as it allows every player to be involved in a skill straight away rather than waiting for their turn at the basket. I always like to teach shooting components without the ball first as the weight of a basketball can certainly make things difficult for young players at first. I explain to the players that shooting the layup is important as it is the running shot so you don't have to stop and then shoot which can allow defenders from behind to catch up and stop you shooting or fouling you, forcing you to shoot two free throws a lot further away from the ring. Have each player place their shooting thumb in the hollow of their opposite hand, I then get them to take one step with their left foot and bring their right knee up and simulate the shooting action. A good friend of mine and coach taught that imagine you had a string attached from your shooting elbow to the same side knee and just like a puppet when the hand moves up to shoot the ball the knee drives up at the same time. The knee driving up is really the power base for the shot similar to the set shot and it is important for players to coordinate the leg drive with the release of the ball.

Once you have simulated without the ball, have the players now do the same action with the ball. I even get them to say **LEFT** then **UP** as they shoot, which gets them focused on the action needed and as young players have a hard time concentrating, saying and doing works really well for them. It is important here to make sure they are shooting the ball high up on the wall. In my league, we are very lucky in that all Under 9 basketball games are played on eight-foot-high rings instead of the standard ten-foot ring. I tell all the players that it must be up above ring height or it will never have a chance of ever going through the ring. It is also important for them to pick a specific spot on the wall they can use as a target to aim at which is what they will be doing once they are at the basket shooting.

Once the majority of the players have successfully completed several shots high up on the wall and are doing this off the opposite foot to the shooting hand with their knee up, we move to the next phase which is the three-step process **LEFT RIGHT LEFT** for right-handed players and **RIGHT LEFT RIGHT** for left-handed players. The key words really do teach the footwork that is required to complete the layup and initially we do this with no basketballs getting all players to simulate and pretend they have one in their hands. Once they start using the balls I have them do the footwork and shot with no dribble making sure the footwork is correct before we add the dribble. Now coach, never wait until it is exactly perfect before moving to the next step and this is always a great opportunity to have a few of the players demonstrate to the others how the skill should be executed. Once the **LEFT RIGHT LEFT, RIGHT LEFT RIGHT** concept is embedded into the feet we then move to using the basketball with the key words **BOUNCE CATCH SHOT** in line with the footwork. Again, have a player who has picked up the concept well demonstrate this to everyone else just to show that it can be done which also creates a little competition within the group to acquire the same skill as quickly as possible.

From practicing the basic components and fundamentals against the wall we move to the ring again following a process that builds from one step shot to three steps shot with a bounce. This is when you start teaching the players about angles for the shot, which is just as important as the shot itself because a poor angle can result in a poor shot. Now the perfect angle for the shot is 45 degrees in between the split line (basket to basket line that separates the right side from the left side of the court) and the backboard. A good guide for the players is just above the low block which puts them on a perfect 45-degree angle. Once you have established the good angle, the next part is a target to aim for and most backboards either have a black or white square drawn on them. Now if the players are on the 45-degree angle all they need do is hit the line on the side of the square around halfway up with a reasonably soft shot and a consistently made basket will result. I like to teach players to shoot close to the basket shots and to shoot them high and soft as early as I possibly can. "The backboard is my friend" – I will have them repeat this little phrase quite often.

Once players are comfortable with the one step shot, take them out three steps from the basket and repeat the same process they did against the wall, except this time they have a basket and a target to shoot for. Keep repeating the same **KEY WORDS LEFT RIGHT LEFT, RIGHT LEFT RIGHT** and **BOUNCE CATCH SHOT** every time they shoot the ball. **KEY WORDS** are such a great teaching tool and I use them as often as I possibly can with new players and teams. Now you gradually move the players further out from the basket and work on having them create a good rhythm for the shot, slowing down to steady on the last step.

If you have a particularly talented team of kids or they are slightly older beginners, then make them practice their layups on both sides of the body. They will eventually have to do this anyway as they get older because a one-sided player or half player is much easier to guard. They should also practice layups at speed with control.

Once the players are comfortable with shooting layups you can introduce the shot into many multiskilling drills to further develop many skills at the same time. I remember attending a clinic by legendary coach Morgan Wooten many years ago and he told us a few stories and one in particular was about when he first started coaching. He told us he really wasn't that good as a coach in those early days and would spend 45 minutes on practicing layups every session and even though he didn't rate himself as a coach, his team hardly ever missed a layup. This tells you that working with a beginner player will require plenty of basic fundamentals for them to become proficient at their skills.

Set Shot Off The Catch
Once the fundamentals of the set shot are progressing and the players have a solid grasp of understanding grounding the anchor (pivot foot) and jab stepping into their shot, then shooting off the pass is the next step. I like to practice this off several forms of attack. The easiest way is for players to flick pass in the air with a little backspin to themselves advancing to the following.

- **Straight lead** – coming directly to the ball usually off a baseline pass in, back cut or flare.

- **Zigzag Lead** – either cutting to or leading away from the basket and when players make this a habit it will open up so many great shooting options.

- **Lane Run** – When on a fast break running the lane (right or left side of the floor) will open up good angles for layups and catch and shoot opportunities.

Set Shot Off the Dribble – Shooting off the dribble will become an important part of any player's offensive arsenal and as they progress as a player. It will also give them far more opportunities to score. Close to the basket you should work mainly on jump stopping then shooting but as you move further from the basket the stride stop is best way to, one keep better balance and two, get more strength and control in the shot. Right-handed shooters establish the left foot as both the pivot and the anchor for the shot bringing the right foot just front of the left, knees flexed forward and into the **ROLL – UP – SNAP** shooting technique focusing on rhythm and a smooth shot without rushing. For left-handers anchor the right foot and for either right or left-handed players practice off the different types of dribbles that are listed in the dribbling section here. Smart coaches will place their best defensive players on your best shooters so the ability to shoot off the dribble and the pass will certainly help your team score more points and really help kids enjoy the game.

Set Shot Off the Rebound – I cover rebounding in the next section but the most important aspects when shooting off a rebound is

- Maintaining balance

- Shoot a quick shot, not a rushed shot

- Make sure you're not shooting the ball into a defensive player

- If you miss then attempt to rebound again and shoot if possible

- You can use a pump shot fake above the head making the defence jump in the air, shooting over them as they're on the way down

Overhead Set Shot – This shot will be quite valuable for your taller or stronger players and it forces the defence to be right on top of you with a good **SMOTHER** otherwise an open shot should give you a good opportunity to score. The technique here is all about a quick knee bend for more power and a slight bend in the shooting arm and a strong wrist snap, completing the shot using the lift from the legs to shoot the ball on the upward movement of the body. As with any skill it will require a fair amount of work for the players to coordinate and master the technique, but it is a hard shot to block so well worth it.

REBOUNDING

This is one skill that can help your team get extra shots and limit the oppositions shot attempts is rebounding. Being tall is quite an advantage and also having the ability to jump certainly does help, but at the beginner level it is all about desire, position and technique. It is interesting to know that the majority of rebounds in the NBA are taken below the level of the ring even though the bulk of the players have the ability to play well above the ring. This proves rebounding is more about position than height and jumping ability, but height is a definite advantage as is athleticism. Most young players will as beginners try and rebound the ball below the level of the eyes so one point you must constantly emphasise is rebounding (catching the ball) above the head.

Basic Technique – A player should have their feet spread shoulder width apart or slightly wider with knees bent forward over the toes and thumbs pointing to their shoulders with fingers spread ready to receive the ball. Have players step slightly forward bending knees and using arms to thrust up above the head in tandem with the jump. Initially I get the player to clap above their head once, then twice and then three times to work on their timing of jumping and hands coming together above their head while actually in the air. The next phase is to have a player hold a ball in their hands and throw it up above their head and rebound it, working on timing, spreading the feet and chinning the ball at the finish. By chinning the ball, the player needs to keep their elbows up and out to protect the ball from opposition players, this is especially taller players because once they bring the ball down, opposition players can bat it out of their hands and if your player is on the defensive end, this could result in easy shots. If the player is on the offensive end, by chinning the ball they are then in position to go back up with the shot.

Rebounding also called the key word **BOARDS,** can be emphasised to young players with the key phrase **MORE SHOTS – LESS SHOTS**.

More Shots – For you and your team as strong rebounders help teams win games. A great High School coach wanted all his players to be greedy, selfish rebounders, it was the only part of the game where it really is okay to go for it. Coaches also get plenty of complaints from players that they are not getting the ball much or more importantly to them more shots during a game. A great answer for the young player is summed up in two words "OFFENSIVE REBOUND" – this will get you more shots and really help your team along with calming the anxiety of players who as they see it they're not getting the ball.

Less Shots – Almost everyone loves to win and they love a winner and kids are no different to the bulk of the population. Keeping opponents down to one shot rather than multiple opportunities to score will certainly help give your team a chance to be a winner. Now this is certainly not easy to do with beginners but I am a great believer in planting seeds that will bear serious fruit in the future and produce far better results for players and teams. I have stated a few times throughout this book that at the beginner level it's not about winning basketball games but playing winning basketball. Doing things, the right way in so far as executing fundamentals, working together with teammates, respecting opponents and officials and having fun playing a great game is what we are striving for.

FAKES

Fakes will be important once players start to get a handle on basic dribbling, passing and shooting skills. Fakes help shift the defensive player to open up opportunities and create plays to free up players to shoot, pass and drive. Players need to understand that they must sell the fake to the defence so they must find the balance between being too fast and also too slow, the first being too quick for the defensive player to react, the second being too easily stopped and countered. The other important point to faking is to not over extend the fake so that your opponent can get their defensive position back as you're trying to bring the ball back to a position in which you want to drive pass or shoot.

Shot Fake

The first fake I teach is the shot fake, it is the easiest of the fakes and requires little movement to make a defender react. Starting in the triple threat stance a player only needs to bring the ball up to the chin while bending the knees and staring towards the basket. As I tell the players, you only need to look like you're taking a shot and wait for a reaction from the defence before you make a drive, pass or even shoot the ball. This will of course only be effective when a player is within or just outside their shooting range of the basket.

Pass Fake

Pass faking will be the fake a player will use the majority of the time. Again, it's never a full passing motion but a half push with knees slightly bent and looking to put the defensive player off balance to create an opportunity to pass the other way or drive the ball past the defence. Players can also use a slight head fake here giving the impression the ball is being passed in that direction.

Dribble Fake

From the triple threat stance there are several ways in which to dribble fake. A player can drop the ball straight down to below the knee without moving the feet and from here can explode forward either on their strong hand or cross the ball over below their knees to their off-hand and drive. The other option is to thrust the body and ball forward to give the impression I am driving hard in that direction and when the defence backs off the player can shoot, pass and also drive if the defence adjusts and steps forward.

Final Thoughts On Offensive Skills

Parents, you really can help your child accelerate their skill development and enjoyment of the game by working in partnership with the coach. You will be spending quality time with your child or children and may even decide to take up the game yourself, as many parents I have had do, over my many years of involvement in the sport. We have even had whole families create wonderful memories playing together in 3 on 3 competitions in the family divisions at local tournaments. Other memories will be playing in the backyard or on the local school court and this healthy quality time together is priceless.

Coaches, as we move further into training sessions, a firm grasp on basic skills will equip you in becoming a "**Points of Emphasis Coach**" and not one that just runs various drills with little or no instruction or feedback to the players. It is so important that you give constant instruction, feedback and correction as your team moves from drill to drill and this must become a habit for you as the coach. But the first step as a coach is to learn the basic skills and how to teach them, even if you're not so great at actually demonstrating the skill physically, so long as you give decent explanation that the players can follow. As soon as one or a few of the players get a good grasp of what you're teaching, have them demonstrate the skill and this will prove to the other players that it can be done and will promote a little competition within the group to follow this player's lead. Offensive skill, gaining and retaining good fundamentals can keep a kid involved in the sport for a lifetime. The sheer thrill of scoring their first basket at training and then in a game will have them beaming and gaining great confidence and when this is shared with their friends or playing with their families, the enjoyment is far greater.

CHAPTER 3
Essential Defensive Fundamentals

CHAPTER 3
ESSENTIAL DEFENSIVE FUNDAMENTALS

Players will spend at least half the game trying to defend the opposition's basket so teaching them the basics of defence will be important unless you want them to just stand there and watch the opposing team score at will. Now this could happen anyway in the first few weeks but I am big on planting seeds in player's heads that will bear the fruits of greater skill development sooner rather than later. Players with some shortcomings in hand eye coordination so far as offensive skills are concerned *can* make huge contributions to their team on defence. Defence requires no basketball and is far easier to play than offence which requires far more skills to become a well-rounded player as you need to pass, catch, dribble, shoot, rebound, lead and cut and combine these skills with other team members. In contrast on defence it is far simpler as you need to be able to guard the player with the ball and the player without the ball. Of course, this does involve some training which can be overlooked because of the sheer volume of offensive skills that need to be covered. Defence does require concentration and desire to play it and the checklist below covers all the skills beginners needed to become good defenders and make positive contributions to their team.

DEFENCE CHECKLIST
- **Starting Point**
- **Stance**
- **Footwork**
- **Position**
- **Smother**
- **Help Defence**
- **Pressure Defence**

STARTING POINT AND UNDERSTANDING

The starting point of defence is simple recognition that the team is on defence. Players must first be taught the simple concept that when our team has the ball we are on offence and when the other team has the ball we are on defence and when neither team has the ball we need to get after it and be first to it. Many a time we have separated players into two teams for a modified game situation and on a side ball every player is waiting for the pass to come to them. This should not take too long and the quicker players learn this the easier defence will be to teach and for them to learn the concepts and components that will make the team better.

STANCE

The stance forms the basis of the start of playing defence and is one of the **KEY WORDS** I use when players are establishing their positions in readiness to play defence. Players must take an open stance with their feet wider than their shoulders place their arms outward for better balance, bend the knees and keep the head centred between the feet with a straight back. Another thing I have players do is extend their left foot forward as the majority of players are naturally right-handed and by having the left foot forward in the stance forward it establishes a position of strength that has the defender ready to push the offensive player with the ball to their weaker hand. This is a process of time but it will bear fruit in the longer term as players once past the beginner level start to think more strategically and begin to push opponents away from their strengths and towards their weaknesses.

FOOTWORK

Once a defensive stance is established, I then start the process of combining the footwork needed to play defence as an individual and eventually as a team. I have all the players line up on the baseline in a defensive stance facing the back wall and then get them to pitter-patter their feet as fast as they possibly can which is like tap dancing on the balls of their feet (heels off the floor) raising each foot just off the floor in a vibrating fashion. I have them do this for 15 to 20 seconds then we start the players working in a zigzag pattern down the floor teaching them to not bounce up and down like a kangaroo, and to keep the feet open and not coming together or crossing at any time while moving backwards. On the change of direction, I show the players how to drop step with the lead foot to change direction to the left or right. Some coaches and basketball skills books teach the step and slide method of defence which means moving one foot while dragging the other behind it, but I prefer quick feet pushing off the left to move right and pushing off the right to move left. Encourage the players to keep their eyes up and not look down at their feet as they are zigzagging. To help this you can have them look at you as you point in the direction you want them to slide by standing in front of the team and have them focus on good stance, quick feet, fast drop steps on the change of direction. Really focus on the **KEY WORDS Stance, Stay Low, Quick Feet** and later **Back, Matchup, Stop Ball** and **Cover** which will become staples especially when working with beginners.

SMOTHER

The easiest way I have found to guard against opponents getting easy shots once players have a reasonable understanding of position is to teach young beginner players to defend their opponents' shots especially close to the basket. Most of the time coaches will yell hands up, hands up as I did for so many years only to watch time and time again easy baskets scored against the team. The biggest problem I have had with hands up is that just holding hands in the air will be quite useless if the distance is not close to the shooter or there could be a gap where the shot can still find an easy path to the basket. Eventually players will understand how to defend in time but this can be accelerated with a simple training technique and **KEY WORD** I call the "**SMOTHER**" which by the very word means to get all over the player with the ball allowing no room to shoot. We also use this technique to smother the player that picks up their dribble to make it hard for them to pass but it is far more effective on a shot as this is only taken in one position facing the basket at the beginner level of play.

The best way we have found to teach the smother is straight after we do our basic footwork drills. First, we pair the players up and have them face each other about one to two metres apart usually along the baseline and into the court. We start the drill without a ball and have one-line stand in a shooting stance and then shout out "**SMOTHER**" to signal the other line stand up close to the shooter with hands stretched up as high as they can and fingers slightly spread and curled over towards the offensive players. After a few seconds, we back the defensive players up and then have them stand in a shooting stance and their teammates follow the same process again to the coach or coaches yelling "**SMOTHER**". Eventually we add a basketball and the players are encouraged to get as close as possible without pushing or touching the player with the ball but smothering the shooter as much as possible. As I am a big believer in multiskilling by having as many elements as possible while running drills, we eventually build the **SMOTHER** into our footwork warm up drills. The **SMOTHER** has become a really important part of our program and is so much more effective than hands up especially with beginner and inexperienced players. I use it for every player I coach as it really is a great focus for players to adopt so that effective pressure can be applied to your opponents.

POSITION

After the player has established their defensive stance, they need to keep themselves in a position between the player they are guarding and the basket they are protecting. Initially just having players stay with an opposition player will be a task in itself as most players want the ball and you may have times in the first few games where every player on the team is chasing the ball leaving open four others who can get easy shots. I take a slightly different approach when I first coach really young kids in that I get them to keep contact with their player by touching them through entire play phases on defence. This gets them used to staying in contact with one player and touching the player they're guarding slowly conditions them to stick to one player who hasn't got the ball. Guarding the ball will be the easiest part of defence, as the majority of players are motivated when they are close to the ball.

Once players are staying with their player, we then get into the really important part of defence the position in relation to themselves, the player they're guarding and the basket they're defending. For many years, I used the **KEY WORDS MAN–YOU–BASKET** which was something that is pretty universal in basketball and we would drill both boys and girls on the words and their meaning having them repeat this several times over then perform the skills so players would understand the meaning during the game. As coaches we would always emphasise how important position was in stopping the opposition scoring really easy baskets and this worked reasonably well for quite a few years and was a major part of our system in teaching effective defence. One day at training we had one of our mums who had extensive experience as a player and was quite involved in coaching at our club who came out with an even better set off **KEY WORDS, SHE–ME–BASKET.** She coached girls at another club and I really liked it so we adopted this in our girl's program. I also added **HE–ME–BASKET** for our boys program and it's a simple gender specific term that rolls nicely off the tongue and easy for coaches, parents and players to learn.

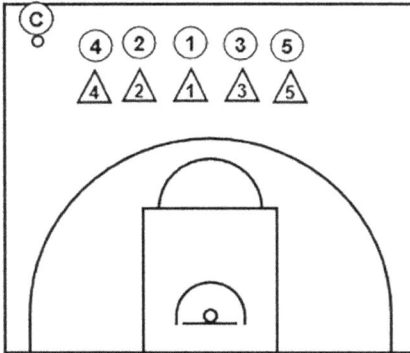

Diagram D1) The easiest way to teach the concept of staying between your player and the basket is to break it down to quarter-court at first by having the offensive players line up across the court and then have the defence line up with the player they're matched up on. It is important that you as much as possible match players up in size and athleticism to start to give players roles so that your smallest players don't get matched up in games against the opposing team's tallest players or players who are not so fleet of foot guarding really quick speedsters who race past them and score. In reality though most players need to understand that they need *to* guard their player only three to four metres from the basket as this will be maximum effective shooting range for most beginner teams and most shots that score will be only one or two metres in distance. Once players really understand that it's the close to the basket shots that hurt our team then they will adjust position backing up to the basket rather than chase out too far and leave big holes for opponents to attack. I use a sequence when teaching defence and it breaks down this way.

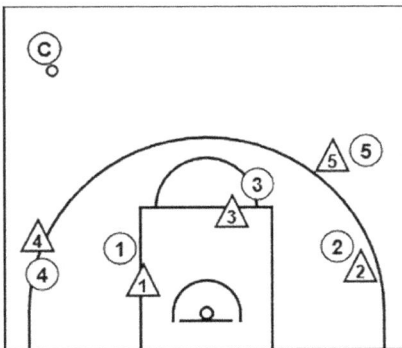

Diagram D2) Once the players are facing each other in a line across the court I start what I call a dry run where by the offensive players cut to the basket then lead out and repeat for 15 – 20 seconds and then offence becomes the defence. All I want the defence to do on this dry run which means a run through without the ball is be close enough to touch their assigned player throughout the play phase. Not using a ball here really helps the defensive players focus on the player they are guarding without the distraction of the ball and it is a good time to introduce **KEY WORDS** for defence **MATCH UP, STANCE, STAY LOW, QUICK FEET**. This works really well but you will need to stop the drill at times to remind a few players that they are too far away from the player they're guarding. I will run this drill for a few minutes and once players are focused on what they are supposed to be doing (I wouldn't wait for perfection here once the majority have the idea move on as time will get away from you and nothing much will be achieved) then I move on to the next step.

The second phase is to introduce the basketball to the drill, and in this situation, the coach makes the first pass after the cutting and leading phase is running for around ten seconds to reinforce every defensive player staying with their player, – now it is time to introduce the ball. It is important to stop the drill when corrections are needed but it is also important to give them time after a coaching correction for the players to work through what they need to do to become good defenders. Some will pick it up quickly others will need time to adjust to new ways of thinking and moving at the same time while being constantly tested. This is also an excellent time to introduce a MAJOR **KEY WORD SMOTHER** into the players' language and it is up to the coach here to take every opportunity to drill the word constantly throughout the training session and then the game. It is a great time to point this out to all players when their teammate does a really good example of the **SMOTHER** and as all good coaches do, they heap praise on great examples to help educate the team and in the hope of multiplying this example into good habits for every player.

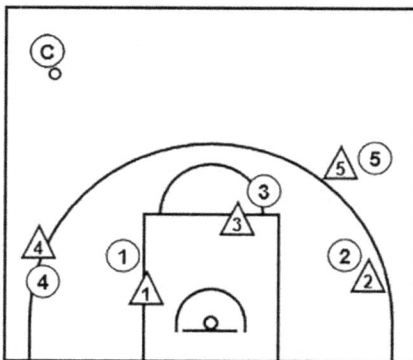

Diagram D3) The third phase is teaching the concept of position, smart angles and a better use of energy. A few weeks into training and games players should have some understanding of the concepts of offence and defence and it is time to further their knowledge. I have all players sit on the halfway line and observe what I call "the 'mad rabbit offensive player'", where I have one of the players run around all over the court with either myself or one of their teammates chasing them everywhere they go like a mad rabbit with no clear direction of what they want to do just run here, there and everywhere as some players do. This is a similar to what they have experienced with the touch technique to a smaller degree than chasing the mad rabbit. Here I stop the drill and make sure all players are standing still and then reposition them as in diagram D4.

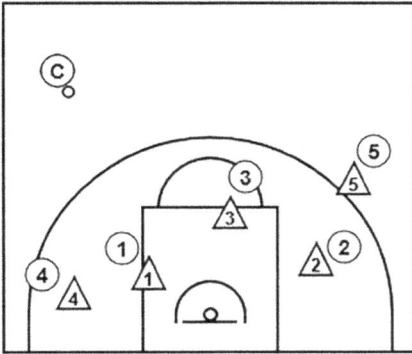

Diagram D4) After correcting players, I ask them to look at where they're positioned along with their teammates. This shows them how to position themselves and not to worry too much when a player receives the ball way out of their shooting range, making sure that your position is always between them and the basket, and they have to play over the top of you, not around you or the worst situation where you're just not there by not picking them up in the first place anyway. You start in the line set-up and have players yell "**HE–ME–BASKET**" or "**SHE–ME–BASKET**" 3-6 times in a row, we do this before every defensive line play and when teams switch from offence to defence. We then dry run without the ball and this time you will be correcting the defensive players every time they are out of position and praising the players who maintain great position. We will from time to time penalise players out of position and sometimes the entire team with a few push-ups to make them all aware that they have to concentrate when playing defence as even one player out of position will give our opposition easy shots.

HELP DEFENCE

At the beginner level help defence will be limited as the task of getting players to stay in the stance in a decent position and to guard the same player will be difficult enough and believe me there will be a huge number of mistakes made as you're building the defence.

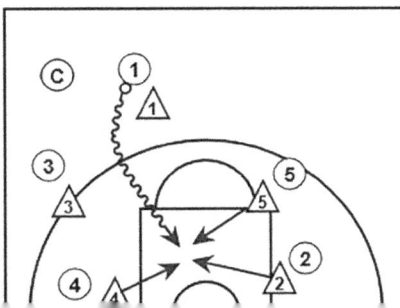

Diagram H1) You can assist the

team by having two to three players as designated safety players whose main role on defence is to protect the basket and still pick up their assigned player, albeit a little looser than their teammates. This player must not venture to far from the key when the ball has passed the centre line and by having two to three safeties you can have one on the court at all times and cover the loss of absent-minded players on game day. It will take several weeks to get the safety player to really understand what they need to do but it is well worth the effort and a little patience and teaching players the safety position will pay big dividends to the team's defence. Most of the time, you'll need to **HELP** on a player that drives the ball hard to the basket or on a hard-cutting player, more so than on a pass.

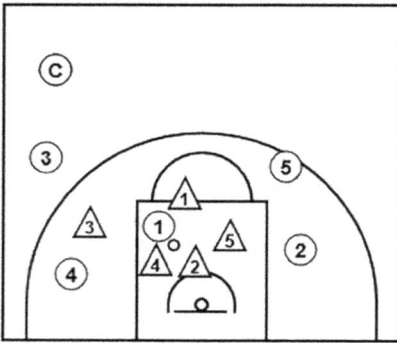

Diagram H2) Of course, you can have every player react to a key word and back up to the basket like help and train them to sink to the basket on a call of **HELP** and attempt to pressure and **SMOTHER** the ball. I don't use this as you will end up with 5 players attempting to **SMOTHER** one player leaving the other four open and a quick pass can lead to really easy scoring opportunities, which will become quite deflating for the team if there is a huge margin in the score so anything, we can do to help stop blow-out games is important. Kids do care about the score and some have a burning desire to win and most want to win especially while competing in a game more so than just training. If your team is not a gifted shooting team as this part of the game can take a while to develop then defence becomes important to being competitive and possibly winning games. Now I constantly emphasise playing winning basketball far more than winning games. We want players to develop good fundamental skills and simple concepts along with plays and teamwork which is a far greater achievement than just winning the game.

PRESSURE DEFENCE

At some point, you may want to play pressure defence with your team and believe me the players will do a merry chase after the ball where ever it is especially when they are beginners in their first season. With this in mind I prefer them to at least do it in a way that will be an advantage to our team and not our opponents. In the previous point on help defence I introduced the safety player and when you play any sort of pressure defence, they will be the most important player on the team even though they have little to do with the pressure component. Now you can certainly pressure up the court with five players and no safety and if your team is really quick and athletic you may have a good chance of stopping a few fast-breaking players who get out ahead of every defender and then shoot uncontested shots.

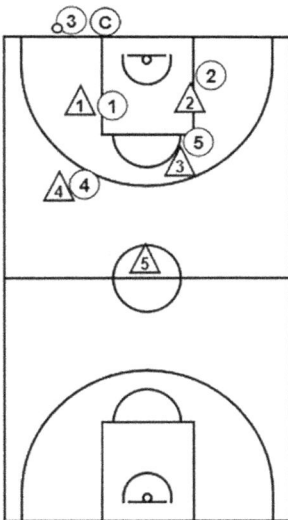

Diagram P1) We never guard the opposition player passing the ball in from the baseline and the **KEY WORDS "IN BOUNDERS"** and **"SAFETY"** are called out which sets our defence up. **IN-BOUNDERS** are the four players without the ball looking to receive the first pass in the court and I want our defenders to mark them as closely as possible making it tough to pass the ball in. The **SAFETY (player 5)** heads back to the middle of the court underneath all opposition players unless one decides to run all the way back to the basket and then the safety can pick them up from the key and you have a loose defender that can double team the player once the ball comes into play. To really apply affective pressure the in-bounders must be guarded as tightly as possible. If the opposition are not good at leading and tend to stand, the result will be many easy steals and opportunities to have more shots.

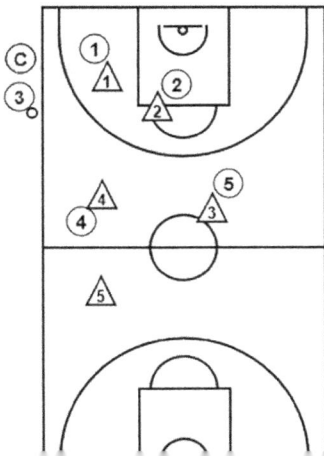

Diagram P2) When the opposition is passing the ball in from the sideline the **SAFETY** needs to position themselves towards the side of the floor where the passer is. As you can see in this diagram player 5 has moved from the middle of the court and hedged towards the sideline. Eventually with a little experience behind them you can teach players to face guard their player which means playing in a direct line between their player and the passer, forcing passes over the top in which the **SAFETY** can pick off and steal. With beginners, the fact that they are reasonably close to an opponent, will be a great starting point along with having a designated player at the back of the defence. This process of guarding **IN-BOUNDERS** with a **SAFETY** can take quite a few weeks into the season but once the players understand their roles it is a great way of pressuring your opponents into poor passes and more opportunities for your team to steal the ball and create more shots.

Diagram P3) & P4) Before you start to pressure up the floor make sure all players can pick up and stay with one opponent in the half and quarter-court otherwise a smart team will penalise a team of ball chasers with quick passes and strong leading which will result in huge scores as players gain more experience and confidence as the seasons progress. In the diagrams, here it shows the **SAFETY number 5** guarding the middle of the key while their teammates play tight on their players on the side ball pass and the **number 5** must guard the basket on any baseline pass. Now if every player could play really great positional defence always on the basket side of their player you wouldn't need a **SAFETY** only **HELP** defence but since we are talking about beginner players it is far wiser to have a **SAFETY**. You could argue that why not play tight on the passer and get up to the line and pressure. Fair point except I teach players passing the ball in to take two steps back which lessens the effect of the player stepping up close to the line and other coaches will often do the same.

P3) Pressure Half-Court – Side   **P4) Half-Court – Baseline**

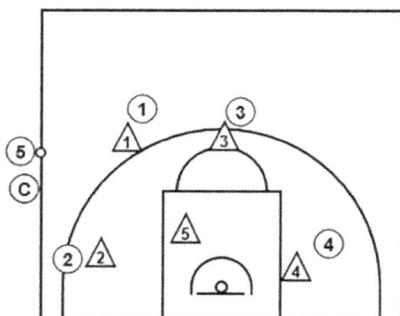

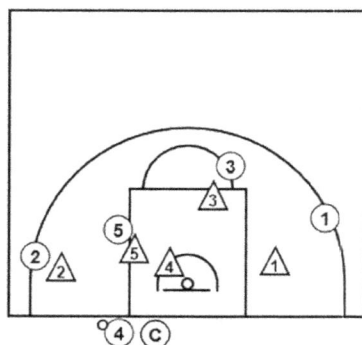

Final Thoughts On Defence

Not all players will develop into great shooters or offensive players and yet they can make such an impact on the game. I often tell the story to the players about Curly a kid I coached many years ago, long before I developed the current system I use. He was a happy go lucky kid with a great nature but had serious coordination problems in that the upper body didn't work so well with the lower body, so offence was really hard for him to get a real handle on, but defence that was his strength. He made our team so much stronger than it really was and we celebrated many trophies in finals as he could basically make life miserable for the opposition's best player. I used to cringe a little when the ball was in his hands as he would often bounce it off his feet, throw terrible passes, make the easiest shot in the game look like an impossible task. I loved his defence though and he was respected for this skill by his teammates and he really found his place in the team. Players spend half the game on defence and it is an area every single player can make a great contribution to the team so time must be spent on all the vital components above. I will not be covering zone defence as it does little to teach kids the necessary defensive skills they are going to need when they eventually become experienced players. My advice is that you become a great teacher of Man to Man and help young players learn valuable footwork, develop better vision, improve teamwork and better concepts.

CHAPTER 4
How To Run And Structure A Training Session

CHAPTER 4
HOW TO RUN AND STRUCTURE A
TRAINING SESSION

GETTING STARTED

Okay coach, you're now armed with your checklist of what you need to teach so far as essential basic skills go and you're ready to start training the team. I cannot stress enough how important good training sessions are to producing not only good players but great teams. Your players will love playing in games far more than training, but training is the place where a player can not only learn skills but also have the opportunity to learn the skills without the pressure of the game riding on its outcome. It is important to understand coach, that the majority of players will do what is comfortable to them when playing in games and be reluctant to try new things. This can be overcome by encouraging players even after a skill they are learning fails time and time again. Eventually they become comfortable and competent and will start using the new skills during games.

SAFETY RULES FOR TRAINING

- **No Jewellery** – The state basketball bodies now have a policy of absolutely no jewellery to be worn in games. It is a common-sense policy that you should adopt at training as nobody wants to see a child get hurt when a simple rule can prevent this.

- **No Food or Chewing Gum** – Now at training I constantly chew gum to keep my mouth and throat moist, but chewing gum is a danger to young players. Gum or any other food can get caught in a young player's throat blocking their airway.

- **No Clothing to be Left on the Floor** – I had a young girl at one of our sessions once slip on a piece of clothing on the floor and was in terrible pain and out 6 weeks with a back injury. Players must respect not only their clothing, but the safety of others by placing clothing in bags or on benches.

- **No Water on the Court** – There is nothing more dangerous than water on a shiny wooden floor. Players must keep water bottles away from doorways or anywhere they can be tripped on or kicked over. No water fights, a good opportunity here to teach players respect for a precious resource.

- **Shoelaces Must be Tied** – Coaches should always be on the lookout for shoelaces dragging on the floor. This is one area I have always been diligent in and still accidents can happen. Halfway through a training session I called the squad to come in for more instructions. I looked up and found a young player lying on the floor in a crumpled mess and in quite a lot of pain. He had fractured his elbow and would not be able to play sport for eight weeks, the culprit an untied shoelace.

- **Fingernails Must be Trimmed** – Check nails before training starts (carry nail clippers in your first aid kit to deal with problem nails). With players closely guarding each other in a confined space like a basketball court it is important that finger nails be kept trimmed. Scratches on skin heal pretty quickly, but damage to an eye can last a lifetime.

- **No Long Plaits or Braided Pony Tails** – A simple rule that stops hair being used as a whip that can hurt teammates and opposition players. Either have these tight to the head, in an open pony tail or wear a head band.

- **Mouth Guards** – I recommend that all players wear mouth guards. It is however a decision parents must make for their children, with some waiting for their child to lose their baby teeth first. There are several types you can purchase, from off the shelf, to custom made ones provided by dentists.

- **No Shorts with Pockets** – This is a danger where players can catch their thumbs on their own pockets leading to painful injuries, having had dislocated and bent back thumbs myself; this is one injury you really want to avoid where possible. Just have your players pull their pockets out the same thing with jacket and tops with side pockets.

- **No Bare Feet** – No bare feet under any circumstances and that includes thongs and open toed sandals at training and street shoes must not be worn as they mark up the court unless you're training outdoors.

ESTABLISHING DISCIPLINE

Having participated in so many training sessions as both player and coach and having observed just as many, several things must be present in order to create a learning environment. Establishing discipline would be the number one priority for every coach, for without it very little will be learnt and training will be a waste of time for all concerned. The last thing you need as a coach is a bunch of wild kids disrupting the session and not concentrating on what you want and need to teach them.

One specific technique I use pretty much with every team I work with to establish discipline and take complete control of the session from the very start is to call a **"time out"** asking players to come to me. Now the first time I do this I usually get most of the players strolling in at a rather slow walking pace and I wait until every player moves into the huddle. From here I give them the **"every basketball player needs to develop hustle"**, speech and when I call a time out, they must rush in, I then ask them to go back to their original position before I called the time out. I ask the players to do five to ten push-ups depending on which age group I am working with. Once they complete the push-ups, I then call time out again and tell them to hustle in, most players respond quickly and do rush in, but there are always a few that tend to take their time. I repeat the same quote that players to become a great basketball player need to hustle and again send them back to the same starting position and again ask for the five to ten push-ups to be done again. You will usually get a few moans and groans, from players especially the ones who did hustle in, but I then explain this is a team game and everyone needs to hustle to help the team perform at its best.

After completing the second set of push-ups I call time out for a third time and this time everyone usually comes in at close to top speed and this is where I tell them that was pretty good but I need just a little more effort, and again send them back to do another set of push-ups. After this process is done every time, I call a time out or ask players to move anywhere they do it by hustling to the place as quickly as they can. This small technique establishes two things, one you require players to move as quickly as they can and hustle and that you are in charge of the training session and two, we are all here to learn how to play basketball.

Push-ups are a minor penalty I favour as it is quick and doesn't waste too much training time, it also serves to increase the strength of the players over a period of time and I will aim for at least 40 to 50 push-ups spread out over a session. You will find that some of the players you're working with will have very poor upper body strength and some will find it a difficult task just to shoot a basket. I find after six to eight weeks of including this type of strength work into every training session the players are comfortable shooting the ball from the free throw line which they will need if fouled in the act of shooting during the game. The increased strength will also improve the passing, rebounding along with better control when shooting and dribbling. I also make it clear to players that although this is a minor penalty it is also a serious part of building up our strength to become better players.

COMMUNICATION

For effective communication, we need to understand that we are all different and everyone has different ways of interpreting things that are said to us, especially young athletes who find it hard to concentrate at the best of times. An example of this would be giving a verbal instruction to a squad of players and everyone could have a different view on the information you're trying to impart to them. As a coach, I am always asking questions of players to find out where they're at in their thinking and understanding of everything that is being taught.

The following is a great guideline and will serve you well if adopted.

Athletes Learn:	Laws of Learning
10% when they hear	Explanation
20% when they see	Demonstration
70% when they do	Repetition

With any explanation keep it as brief and as simple as possible, then demonstrate it using key words as much as possible. Now remember coach it doesn't have to be a perfectly executed demonstration which is easy for me as an experienced player, but you may never have played the game yourself. Demonstrate it as well as you can or ideally have someone who has played the game for a few seasons help you out at the first couple of training sessions, until you feel you have a good handle on things. Once you have any player in your team that can demonstrate a skill then always use them as the prime example. This will create some minor competition within the group as teammates also want to be able to do the skill just as well as the demonstrator. Even though I can show the players exactly what I want I will always use their teammates where ever possible as they will take the attitude it is easy for you coach you have played for many years.

In this early development of the team the communication will mainly be one way with you explaining, correcting and then summing up how individuals and the team has done during the drill and the session. I do however from time to time ask questions of various players and the group to see where their understanding is at in relation to skills, drills and simple plays.

STRUCTURING THE SESSION

Every training session needs a simple guideline or plan to keep the players focused on the essential basics they need to learn. It is always a good idea to write down what you are planning to do for the entire session with a time limit for each skill and drill you need to cover. Setting time limits will stop you spending too much time on just one basic skill while sacrificing several other important basic skills that need to be covered. Most coaches are guilty of this at some point where you get so caught up with making sure a skill is perfect or that they truly understand the drill and it is working as it should, in the meantime everything that was originally planned is now lost as training was spent primarily on one aspect of the game when at this age group everything is important and time should be equally divided. A quick list is better than nothing at all and it can be as simple as writing down a few skills to be covered and some simple drills along with some time spent on a glaring weakness during your last game.

TRAINING SESSION GUIDELINES
- **Footwork drills**
- **Passing and leading**
- **Dribbling**
- **Shooting**
- **Transition**
- **Basic Plays**
- **Defensive concepts**
- **Modified scrimmage**

Eventually once you and your players gain some experience you can multiskill, combining as many of points 1)-2)-3)-4) and working on two to even six skills in the one drill. It is really important that the players do things correctly even if you have to slow them down to make sure they execute basic fundamentals. Remember you are continuously teaching coach, not just letting them go through the motions of running a drill. Feedback is really important to young players and the more you can give them in positive direction, the better your team will function on the court.

Have set times for skills and drills that you run and, coach, don't worry if it's not perfect or if your players are having a hard time understanding on that very day. I find that if they have the general idea then you can build on this the next time you have training. This is not a race to be perfect, and with kids at this age they will surprise you one minute with their progress and no doubt disappoint when you think they have forgotten most of the things you're trying to teach them. These memory lapses will be fleeting and a little persistence and patience on your behalf will bring positive results so long as your training structure is clear and consistent along with the instructions. Keeping drills short and sharp will allow you and the players to cover everything needed to build a team in a short period of time. Some coaches are very stubborn and want something run or executed perfectly and sacrifice so many other aspects of what their players and team needs and then are dumbfounded when their progress is slow and unproductive. Keep it simple and quick coach and if it's looking pretty bad, get out of it and move on to another drill. You can always come back the next session and modify it down further to help players have a small victory over something that they didn't quite understand last time around.

As you are working with very young and inexperienced players there is no need for the type of training session that an experienced team of many years would do. Simple break downs of the essential skills and simple plays, is all that is needed and the next section will give you detailed training plans and drills to run well-structured effective training sessions.

TRAINING PLANS

A training plan can be as simple as a few drills marked on a piece of scrap paper to an organised training diary filled with court diagrams and complex training drills based on scouting opponents' reports. Luckily at the beginner level it is simply making sure all the players on the team get to practice all the basic skills both on offence and defence. I always have a sequence to training beginner players and for the most parts cover every possible skill these players will need in order to be effective players and eventually a team. I like to block training in three, five- and ten-minute drills depending on timeframes of 45-minute, one hour or more time and whether you have a full or half court to work on.

First Training Session
At this first training session it is important to introduce the players to the core skills needed to play, along with some rules. It is also a time to establish a fair amount of discipline to make all players realise they are now part of a team. Water breaks will be determined by the weather conditions of the day, two to three in cooler and four to six in warmer conditions.

4.00 – 4.05 – Warm Ups Footwork
- Zigzags sharp changes of direction side-line to side-line
- **SLOW ZIG – FAST ZAG** with a target hand off a hesitation stutter step
- Defensive slides
- **MATCHUP** Zigzag with a partner one on offence, one on defence no ball
- **MATCHUP SMOTHER** – add ball after technique is established

4.05 – 4.10 – Dribbling
- Stationary dribbling working on technique with both hands, eyes up
- Line Drill adding various dribbles

4.10 – 4.15 – Passing, Catching, Pivoting and Dribbling
- Stationary passing in pairs
- Dribble to the free throw line-jump stop-pivot-pass. Vary dribbles and passes

Drink Break

4.15 – 4.20 – Shooting Technique
- Shooting technique
- Layups technique

4.20 – 4.25 min – Shooting
- Two-line layup drill
- Spot shooting to three or five baskets

4.25 – 4.30 – Shooting off the dribble and pass
- Three-lines shooting of the dribble – first to three or five
- **SLOW ZIG, FAST ZAG** lead with target hand catch and shoot – first to three or five

Drink Break

4.30 – 4.35 – SPLIT (concept of creating space)
- Three-man **SPLIT** off the defensive rebound bump drill
- Five-man **SPLIT** off the defensive rebound bump drill

4.35 – 4.40 min – Advantage and Transition
- Two on one quarter-court
- Three on two quarter-court

4.40 – 4.50 – Half Court 5 on 5 Game
- **MATCHUP** line drill – touch defence, **SPLIT** and zigzag offence dry run no ball
- **MATCHUP** line drill – touch defence, **SPLIT** and zigzag offence dry run with ball

Drink Break

4.50 – 5.00 – Scrimmage (Game)
Modified scrimmage, explain rules as you go and introduce the **KEY WORDS** the players will eventually respond to. The Coach can limit dribble to involve more players, create specific match ups and also no stealing the ball unless it's from the player you're matched up on to give everyone a chance to enjoy the game.

- Warm down, walk, stretch and a post training address going over important points we practiced at training, finishing with hands in team chant.

Second Training Session
After the first game, you will have a better idea of how quickly players are progressing in their understanding of the rules, their many weaknesses and some strengths. At the first session, you tend to spend most of the session explaining drills and skills even though the players will forget 90% of what was said and taught to them at that first session if a week has gone by. Everything should move forward a little faster each week, as players are comfortable with familiar drills and are building on skills. I usually run a similar session to the first and I certainly inject more **KEY WORDS** and a few extra drills if players are making progress.

4.00 – 4.05 – Warm Ups Footwork
- Zigzags sharp changes of direction side-line to side-line
- **SLOW ZIG** – **FAST ZAG** with a target hand off a hesitation stutter step
- Defensive slides
- **MATCHUP** Zigzag with a partner one on offence, one on defence no ball
- **MATCHUP SMOTHER** – add ball after technique is established

4.05 – 4.10 – Dribbling
- Stationary dribbling working on technique with both hands, eyes up
- Line drill adding various dribbles

4.10 – 4.15 – Passing, Catching, Pivoting and Dribbling
- Stationary passing in pairs
- Dribble to the free throw line-jump stop-pivot-pass. Vary dribbles and passes

Drink Break

4.15-4.20 – Shooting Technique
- Shooting technique
- Layups technique

4.20 – 4.25 min – Shooting
- Two-line layup drill
- Spot shooting to three or five baskets

4.25 – 4.30 – Shooting off the dribble and pass
- Three-lines shooting of the dribble – first to three or five
- **SLOW ZIG**, **FAST ZAG** lead with target hand catch and shoot – first to three or five

Drink Break

4.30 – 4.35 – Split (concept of creating space)
- Three-man **SPLIT** off the defensive rebound bump drill
- Five-man **SPLIT** off the defensive rebound bump drill

4.35 – 4.40 min – Advantage and Transition
- Two on one quarter-court
- Three on two quarter-court

4.40 – 4.50 – Half-court Five on Five Game
- Matchup Line drill – touch defence, **SPLIT** and zigzag offence dry run no ball
- Matchup Line drill – touch defence, **SPLIT** and zigzag offence dry run with ball

Drink Break

4.50 – 5.00 – Scrimmage (Game)
Modified scrimmage, explain rules as you go and introduce the key words the players will eventually respond to. The Coach can limit dribble to involve more players, create specific match ups and also no stealing the ball unless it's from the player your matched up on to give everyone a chance to enjoy the game.

- Warm down, walk, stretch and post-training address where we go over important points we practiced at training and finish with hands in team chant.

Third and Fourth Training Sessions
A few training sessions and games now and the players should be starting to have a basic (certainly not full) understanding of rules and that when we are on offence, we are attacking the basket on one end and defending on the other end. Here I start to add a baseline play **SNAKES** and build more multiskill training for the team. I also want to create more game situation training so we are helping players get ready for not only what they face during the game, but how we want them to play, so I like to stop the play and explain what I want players to do and how to position themselves.

4.00 – 4.05 – Warm Ups Footwork
- Zigzags sharp changes of direction side-line to side-line
- **SLOW ZIG – FAST ZAG** with a target hand off a hesitation stutter step
- Defensive slides
- Matchup Zigzag with a partner one on offence, one on defence
- Matchup **SMOTHER** with a ball

4.05 – 4.10 – Dribbling
- Dribble Knockout

4.10 – 4.15 – Passing, Catching, Pivoting and Dribbling
- Dribble free throw line-jump stop-pivot-pass. Vary dribbles and passes

Drink Break

4.15 – 4.30 – Shooting Technique & Shooting
- Shooting technique
- Layups technique
- Three-lines shooting of the dribble – first to three or five
- **SLOW ZIG, FAST ZAG** lead with target hand catch and shoot – first to three or five

Drink Break

4.30 – 4.35 – SNAKES into SPLIT
- **SNAKES** out of bounds play into **SPLIT**

4.35 – 4.40 – Advantage and Transition
- Two on one half court tap drill
- Three on two half court tap drill

4.40 – 4.50 – Half Court Five on Five Game
- Keepings off working on **SPLIT** and strong passing and leading
- Matchup Line drill – touch defence, **SPLIT** and **ZIGZAG** leading offence with the ball and if the ball goes out over the baseline run **SNAKES**

Drink Break

4.50 – 5.00 – Scrimmage (Game)
Modified scrimmage, explain rules as you go and introduce the **KEY WORDS** the players will eventually respond to. The coach can limit dribble to involve more players, create specific match ups and also no stealing the ball unless it's from the player you're matched up on, giving everyone a chance to enjoy the game. Use the **SNAKES** out of bounds play for practice and make sure you intentionally set a few of these plays up just for the practice.

- Warm down, walk, stretch and post training address where we go over important points we practiced at training, While the players are stretching you can have the player watch you explaining the **SNAKES** play on your coaching board, as well as defensive positioning. The more you emphasise this the more the player will understand and at this stage you're more planting seeds for the future. As always, we finish with an all hands in team chant.

Fifth and Sixth Training Sessions

After a month of training sessions and games, players should have a better understanding of rules and be reacting to the main **KEY WORDS**. The **SPLIT** and the baseline play **SNAKES** should be coming along and the team defence should be building with a **SAFETY** player, the **SMOTHER,** along with the concept of staying with a player and not just chasing the ball. Time to add more multiskill training for the team and I also introduce a side ball play called **LINE,** to give players a focus when we are passing in from the side. Keep creating more game situation training and it is here I start asking the players basic questions to see where their thinking and understanding of what is being taught is at.

4.00 – 4.05 – Warm Ups Footwork
*   Zigzags sharp changes of direction side-line to side-line
*   **SLOW ZIG – FAST ZAG** with a target hand off a hesitation stutter step
*   Defensive slides
*   Matchup **ZIGZAG** with a partner one on offence, one on defence
*   Matchup **SMOTHER** with a ball

4.05 – 4.20 – Passing, Catching, Pivoting and Dribbling and Shooting
*   Dribble free throw line-jump stop-pivot-pass. Vary dribbles and passes
*   Shooting and layup technique quick review
*   Two-man combination drills

Drink Break

4.20 – 4.30 – Shooting
*   Rebound and Shoot
*   Three-lines fake and drive around cones or chairs dribble

4.30 – 4.40 – SNAKES / LINE into SPLIT
*   **SNAKES** baseline out of bounds play into **SPLIT**
*   **LINE** side ball play into **SPLIT**

Drink Break

4.40 – 4.45 – Advantage and Transition
*   Two on one half court tap drill
*   Three on two half court tap drill

4.40 – 4.50 – Half Court Five-on-Five Game
- Keepings off working on **SPLIT** and strong passing and leading
- Matchup Line drill – touch defence, **SPLIT** and **ZIGZAG** leading offence with the ball and if the ball goes out over the baseline run **SNAKES**

Drink Break

4.50 – 5.00 – Scrimmage (Game)
Modified scrimmage, explain rules as you go and introduce the **KEY WORDS** the players will eventually respond to. The coach can limit dribble in order to involve more players, create specific match ups and also no stealing the ball unless it's from the player you're matched up on, giving everyone a chance to enjoy the game. Use the **LINE** and **SNAKES** out of bounds play and make sure you intentionally set a few of these plays up just for the practice. Add pressuring **IN-BOUNDERS** with a **SAFETY** player.

- Warm down, walk, stretch and post training address where we go over important points we practiced at training. While the players are stretching you can have them watch you explain **LINE**, **SNAKES** play on your coaching board, as well as defensive positioning, the **SAFETY** and pressuring the **IN-BOUNDERS**. As always, we finish with an all hands in team chant.

Seventh and Eighth Training Sessions
If your players are older beginners around the ten to eleven age bracket you will certainly see a big difference appearing now in their teamwork and the **KEY WORDS** should be making a huge difference to their performance. If the players are younger you will need a little more time for the **KEY WORDS** to really take hold, but all teams and players are different and some will amaze you and others maybe a little frustrating but your persistence with the system will be rewarding as it has for me over many years.

4.00-4.05 – Warm Ups Footwork
- **Zigzags** sharp changes of direction side-line to side-line
- **SLOW ZIG – FAST ZAG** with a target hand off a hesitation stutter step
- Defensive slides
- Matchup offence **ZIGZAG** movement without running past the defender, on the coaches whistle several times down the floor both players stop so we can practice the **SMOTHER** a ball can be added to the drill up also

4.05-4.25 – Passing, Catching, Pivoting and Dribbling and Shooting
- Keepings off
- Full court layup drill
- Two-man combination drills

Drink Break

- Rebound and Shot
- Three-lines fake and drive around cones or chairs dribble

4.25 – 4.35 – SNAKES / LINE into Split
- **SNAKES** baseline out of bounds play into **SPLIT**
- **LINE** side ball play into **SPLIT**

4.35 – 4.45 – Advantage and Transition
- Three-man weave Two on One full court
- Three on Two half court tap drill

Drink Break

4.40 – 4.50 – Half-Court Five 0n Five Game
- Matchup Line drill – touch defence, **SPLIT** and **ZIGZAG** leading offence with the ball and if the ball goes out over the baseline run **SNAKES** and also **LINE** from the side ball, setting this up at the centreline to start the play

Drink Break

4.50 – 5.00 – Scrimmage (Game)
Modified scrimmage, explain rules as you go and introduce the **KEY WORDS** the players will eventually respond to. The coach can limit dribble to involve more players, create specific match ups and also no stealing the ball unless it's from the player you're matched up on, giving everyone a chance to enjoy the game. Use the **LINE** and **SNAKES** out of bounds play and make sure you intentionally set a few of these plays up just for the practice. Add pressuring **IN-BOUNDERS** with a **SAFETY** player.

- Warm down, walk, stretch and post training address where we go over important points we practiced at training, While the players are stretching you can have the players come and explain **LINE**, **SNAKES** play on your coaching board to their teammates as well as defensive positioning, the

SAFETY and pressuring the **IN-BOUNDERS**. As always, we finish with an all hands in team chant.

Depending on your team and their age, there is a full range of drills in the next chapter to choose from and you can insert them into the time blocks to suit your skill level and learning ability of the players.

Fun Training Session

We always throw in a fun session during the season and insert fun drills into regular training sessions from time to time just to break up the routine and give the players a mental break. You can also start and end training with a fun drill which will have the players smiling and laughing and after all, coach, it's only a game to young kids and we can forget this sometimes when involved in competitive games in a league. I usually start out with a simple concentration drill and build this up as the session continues and allocate a few minutes to each drill.

A full list and explanation of fun drills we use is located in Chapter 5

- In – Out
- Two-man Face Tag
- Two-man Knee Boxing
- Thomas the Tank Drill
- Chain Tag
- Octopus
- Shark
- Two ball Knockout
- Dribble Races
- Any Competitive Team and Individual Shooting Drill
- Numbers
- Tunnel Ball
- Two on two, three on three mini tournaments
- Scrimmage – players love playing the game this time with minimal coaching so they have freedom to make their own choices here the coach is the referee

A full list of the drills I use are all in the next chapter and if your team can only use a half-court that's okay, just have the players touch the halfway line and come back simulating playing on a full court. I have listed many half-court drills that you can insert and I am sure that there are many you will add your own modifications to and tailor the training session to your particular team and age group.

CHAPTER 5
Simple And Effective Training Drills

CHAPTER 5
SIMPLE AND EFFECTIVE TRAINING DRILLS

Drills will form an important part of structuring a team's training session, the following drills I feel are both simple and appropriate for beginner players and for when they have some experience to advance their skills. What I tend to do with beginner players and teams is keep the drills familiar and add extra skills and components to something they're comfortable with. I will do this with many of the drills here by showing the basic drill and then show how I modify the drill to include more skills and sometimes less, to help players learn to play and develop. Do change the drills from time to time to keep it fresh for the players.

CHECKLIST

Diagram Key – Shows all the key symbols used in all the diagrams

Footwork Drills
* Offensive Zigzags
* Offensive **SLOW ZIG – FAST ZAG** (with target hand up)
* Defensive slides Zigzags Quick Feet
* Matchup Two-players One on Offence, One on Defence Reaction Drill
* Matchup Two-player Zigzags (including smother and pivoting)

Passing Drills
* Stationary Two-player Drill (working on basic passing technique)
* Two-handed Chest, Bounce, Overhead Pass
* One-handed Step to the Side Bounce, Baseball Pass
* Concentration Passing
* Two-line Pass and Move
* Three-line Pass Inside Out In
* Three-man Weave
* Five-man Weave

Pressure Passing Drills
* Three-man Pass and Pressure
* Three-man Pressure the **IN-BOUNDER**

- Monkeys in the Middle
- Square Passing Drill

More passing drills located in Chapter 6 that relate to building the **SPLIT**

Dribbling Drills
Important that every player has a ball at training or at a minimum one ball per two players.

Straight line dribbling to the centre line on strong hand and back on the opposite hand
- Basic and Creative Dribbles
- Dribble Races
- Using Cones and Props
- Attack and Pullback Drill
- Dribble Knockout
- Face Off
- Shark
More Dribbling Drills in the Fun Drills Section

Shooting
- Two-line Layup Drill
- Layup Races (including various shots)
- Spot Shooting (competitive)
- Three-line Drive Attack the Defence (Cone)
- Three-line Fake, Step Around, Drive and Shot
- Two-ball knockout
- Pressure Spot Shooting
- **BOARDS** and Shoot
- **BOARDS** Shot Outlet Layup

Combination (2+ skills in the same drill)
- Baseline Dribble, Pivot, Pass
- Sideline Dribble, Pass, Lead
- Pass Exchange, Drive and Score
- Two-line Multiskill Layup Drill
- Two-man Half-court Series
- Quick Pass, Lead and Shoot
- Full Court Layup Drill – Added Defensive Options

Advantage and Transition Drills

- Quarter-court Two-on-One
- Quarter-court Three-on-Two
- Half-court Two-on-One Coach Tags Defender
- Half-court Three-on-Two Coach Tags Defenders
- Full Court Three-man Weave Two-on-One
- Full Court Five-man Weave Three-on-Two
- Half-court Three-man Weave Two-on-One
- Half-court Five-man Weave Three-on Two

Fun Drills

- In Out
- Two-man Tag & Knee Boxing
- Thomas the Tank
- Chain Tag
- Octopus
- Shark
- Numbers
- Coach Says
- Tunnel Ball

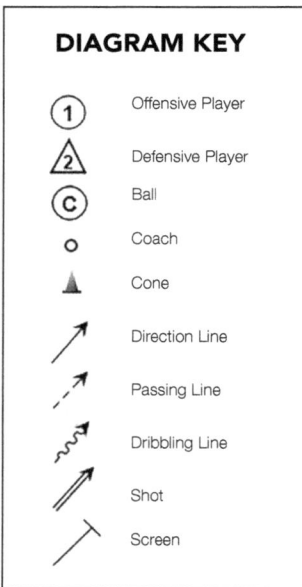

DIAGRAM KEY

Symbol	Description
①	Offensive Player
△2	Defensive Player
©	Ball
○	Coach
▲	Cone
↗	Direction Line
↗	Passing Line
↗	Dribbling Line
↗	Shot
⟍	Screen

Diagram Key

For those new to basketball the symbols on diagrams could be slightly confusing especially the different arrowed lines, but this Diagram Key will help you understand what is happening on the court along with a description for all the diagrams, explaining the drills and the many variations and options a coach has.

FOOTWORK

"The better the footwork the better the player" is something I have young players repeat as often as possible. A player with good footwork will always get open for the ball and be in better position to guard an opposition player on defence. Remember coaches the players spend the majority of the game without the ball so working on good footwork is never a waste of practice time. If it's important to you coach it will be important to the players.

Zigzags

I always prefer players to use basketball footwork and zigzags are great for warm ups rather than just running in a straight line.

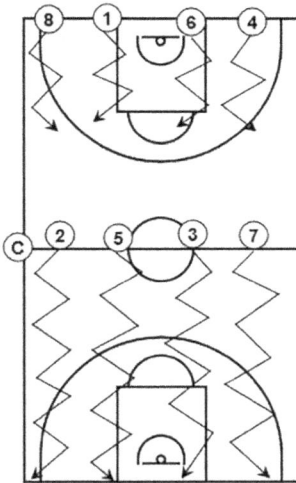

Diagram 1a) A full explanation of footwork technique is in Chapter 2 and the setup here is to start everyone on the baseline. Now with larger squads or multiple teams training together it could be wise to stagger the players, as they may trip and fall as they zigzag their way down the floor. Then again if your team is in need of the contact work to help players get used to this aspect if the game, then reduce the width of the court to force dodging, weaving and contact. The coach can also blow the whistle and the players can stop then start, or add a full circle pivot or pretend rebound jumping in the air clapping above their head for extra practice.

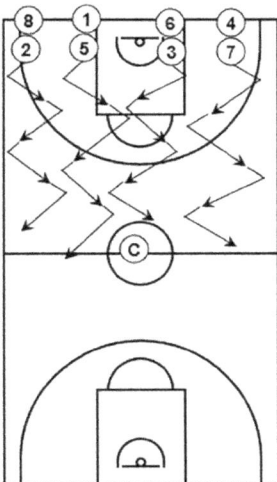

Slow Zig – Fast Zag

This is an important drill that follows the regular zigzags, as it will help get players open for the ball and help your team advance the ball down the court to increase the number of shots players can get in a game.

Diagram 2a) In this drill the players should have some space to complete the cut so they can get a great grounding in an important skill. **SLOW ZIG – FAST ZAG** with a target hand and come to a stop, then practice it the other way. As with the previous drill, you can have players add a pretend catch ball, to the hip protection, full circle pivot

89

and a simulated pass before the next cut. As the players become experienced, I have them do this drill with a ball tossing it up into the air then execute the lead catching the ball placing it on the front of the hip during a full pivot.

Defensive Slides
Approximately half the game is spent on defence and as important as getting the ball down the floor is, stopping opposition baskets will also have a high priority if the team is going to play winning basketball. A full explanation of defensive technique is available at the start of Chapter 3 and explains step by step the correct stance and the building up of components that turns a stand still beginner player into a lock down tough to beat defensive player.

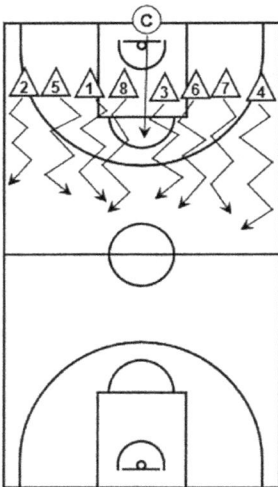

Diagram 3a) Players form a line along the baseline facing the back wall, with the coach in front of the team. After slowly going through correct stance and technique of slide and drop step along with quick feet pitter patter, players head down the court in a zigzag pattern keeping their heads pointed to the front. The coach follows the team down the floor making corrections as they slide. A great way for a coach to make sure players keep their heads up is to point in the direction you want them to slide, this also helps improve reaction time.

Smother and Match-Up

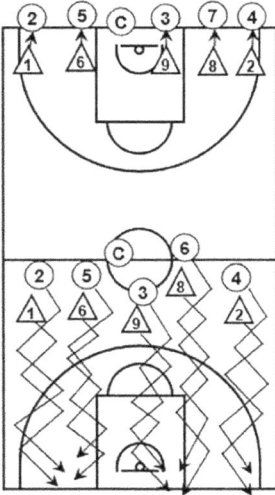

Diagram 4a) Players pair up along the baseline facing each other about two steps apart. From this setup, the coach calls out **SHOT** and **SMOTHER,** with one line simulating a shooting stance while the other line steps up close to their teammate and takes a **SMOTHER** position for a five count then backs off to their original position. Both lines take several turns as offence and defence and it is important that the smothering player is in the correct position so they are not going to be called for a foul and the player simulating the shot holds their ground with arms up, not being intimidated by the player attacking them. Once the **SMOTHER** has had a decent amount of practice, the players are ready to zigzag their way down the court working on both their offensive and defensive footwork. This can be done either in a half or full court drill and once most of the players have a good understanding of technique and position, the coach can call out change or blow the whistle so players then transition from offence to defence similar to what happens in a game situation. I encourage players not to just sprint past the teammate that is guarding them but rather, help their teammate improve their defensive footwork by sharp zigzagging and fakes, which also helps them react better.

PASSING DRILLS

From simple to complex drills, passing forms the backbone of great teamwork and great team players. Make sure you concentrate on both the passing and the catching. I often ask the players at training to solve this small riddle. **"When is a pass not a pass?"** Answer **"When nobody catches it."** It becomes a mere throw when it is not caught so coaches, keep your eye on not only the passing but also on the catching, as the two are vital to any team's successful improvement.

Basic Passing

Starting with this simple static passing drill is always good with beginners and also at distances that will not have players straining to hit their target.

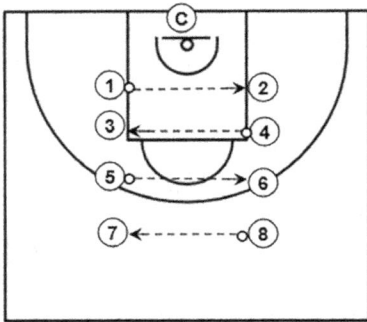

Diagram 1a) Have players pair up several metres apart with one ball per pair. In this drill, you're working on the basic technique of passing and catching and I usually add a touch of competition by having a race to reach a certain number of completed passes. This makes players work a little harder, but the main focus here is correct technique which is covered in **Chapter 2**.

Passes covered here
1. Two-handed chest pass
2. Two-handed bounce pass
3. Two- handed overhead pass
4. One-handed step around bounce pass
5. One-handed baseball pass, for older kids
6. Fake a pass – Make a pass

Concentration Passing
This can be a fun or a frustrating drill where you need a minimum of three players up to a whole team with a target of consecutive passes and you can also create several teams and have a competition again for the completion of a set number of passes.

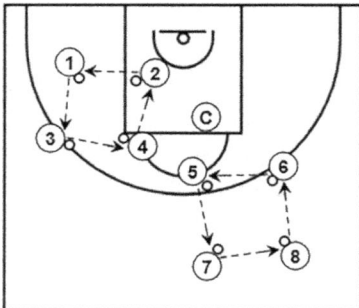

Diagram 2a) In this drill I have divided the team into Four's approximately three metres apart and have them make consecutive passes in both clockwise and anticlockwise directions. For beginners, this may be as low as five or as high as 20 as they become a little more experienced. If any player drops the ball the count goes back to zero and no high lob passes allowed. When I do this drill with the whole team, I give them a time limit to complete the task with a small penalty if not completed.

Two Line Pass and Move

From static passing to learn technique through to movement and footwork passing and receiving, I like this drill as a modified basic introduction to passing and catching while moving.

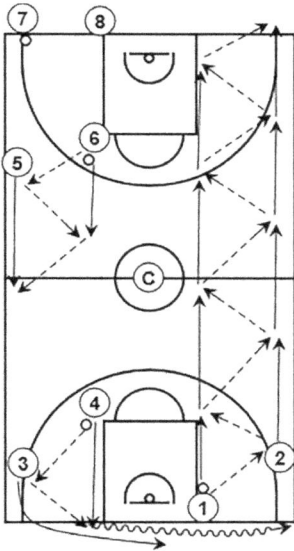

Diagram 3a) Pair players up with one ball per pair starting at the baseline. They move down the floor staying parallel to each other passing the ball slightly forward then running to get slightly in front at least level with their teammate so the ball keeps moving forward down the court. When they reach the end the player with the ball dribbles across the baseline, you can also let the pair veer into the basket and shoot before moving across to the other side of the court. It is also important that players that were on the inside moving down the court on one side must move to the outside lane coming back the other way.

Points of emphasis

- Catch on one-foot pass on the other to avoid travelling
- Keep good spacing and keep moving the ball forward passing slightly ahead of your teammate
- Turn the upper body slightly to receive the ball

Three-line Passing Inside Out In

Diagram 4a) Form three lines on the baseline either using the whole court or as diagrammed here to one side of the basket, with a ball in the centre of the line. The players run down the floor holding their line passing the ball from the inside line to the outside player and back to the player in the middle then on to the outside player on the opposite side and back to the middle again. The drill continues to the end of the court and the players rotate positions so everyone has a turn being in the middle. As in the previous two-man drill, the players can move towards the basket and score before exiting the court off to the baseline. If you're only running the drill down the middle of the court then when the players finish, they run back down the side-line and the player with the ball dribbles back to restart the drill from the same end. The same points of emphasis apply as in the two-line passing drill.

3 Man Weave

This is a very popular drill used by many coaches throughout the world.

Diagram 5a) Form three lines along the baseline, you can also run the drill along either side of the basket like the diagram or down the middle of the court. Either way, the players in the middle line start with the ball. The outside players move ahead of the player with the ball who then can pass to either the player to their left or right. After the pass is made, the passer cuts behind the player who now has the ball and then gets ahead of the player on the opposite side who will receive the next pass. The drill continues down the court until they reach the baseline or they can veer into the basket for a shot at the finish of the weave. This is a great drill to teach players to get out ahead of the ball, to move the ball forward and for emphasising the preventing of travels. You can also change up the passes used as in two and one- handed chest along with bounce passes and make sure players are seeing the ball into their hands on the catch.

Five-man Weave

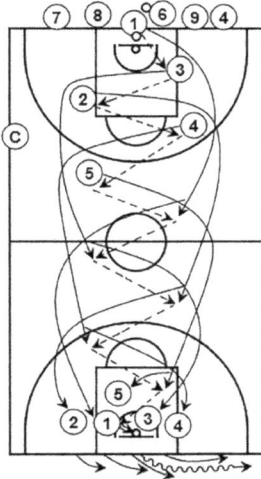

Diagram 6a) The five-man weave is just an extension of the three-man weave but instead of running behind one player after the pass, the player extends this out past two players, still getting out in front of the ball. All the points of emphasis for moving and passing drills apply here and I have the players come directly down the middle of the court. Depending on the size of the team, players can move off the court and run down the sideline back to the start or just return with the same five and weave directly back. I include shooting a shot and rebound until a score is made.

Pressure Passing Drills

Pressure passing drills will add an important skillset that players need to be successful at in the games that they play. Remembering that basketball is the opposite to school in that you are constantly being tested before you learn the lesson, so if we can replicate this at training it helps a player build a great base of tests both at games and then at training, providing them with valuable experience. Run these in combination with the **SPLIT** and keepings off drills, for a good grounding in applying and dealing with pressure while receiving and passing.

3 Man Pass and Pressure

A good drill to follow up on the basic two man passing series covering passing technique and various passes, which can now be put into practice in this and the **SPLIT** drills that also combine keepings off. The use of fakes is really important here.

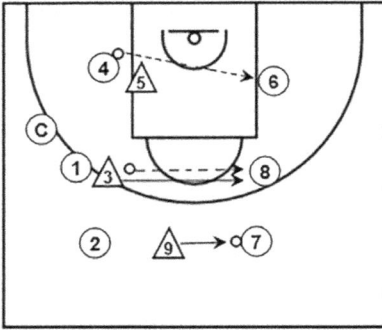

Diagram 1a) Players form teams of three with a ball for each team and with each team spread several meters apart. The player with the ball stands in front of the pair and passes to the single player opposite them. After making the pass the player runs to the player they have passed to and plays pressure defence on them, making it hard for them to make the pass back to their teammate on the opposite side. Once they make a pass, they in turn go and pressure the teammate they have just passed to and the drill continues. The main point of emphasis here are fake high, pass low, fake low, pass high and encourage the defensive player to mirror the ball with their hands.

3 Man Pressure the IN-BOUNDER

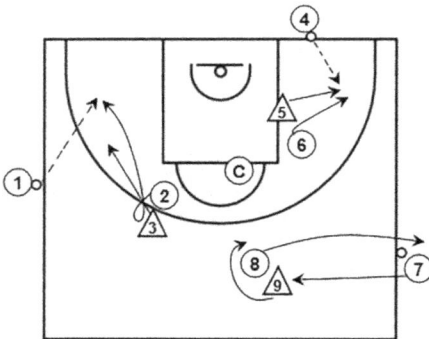

Diagram 2a) Form teams of three players with one ball per team and have the player with the ball start out of bounds making sure they are at least two steps back from the line so they have room to step into the pass without causing a violation by over stepping the line. In this diagram **(1)** is passing to player **(3)** with **(2)** as the defence trying to deflect or steal the ball and it is the same with **(4)** and **(6)** who are the offence and **(5)** the defence. After the play is completed the rotation is as follows- the passer **(7)** becomes the defender, **(9)** the defender becomes the next receiver and **(8)** who was receiving the pass dribbles out of bounds and becomes the passer. This is an important drill as it simulates the first pass to help the team get the ball down the court. I make this drill a little more competitive by adding a small push-up penalty of three to five push-ups for the defence if the pass is successfully made and caught without travelling and the same penalty for both offensive players if the pass isn't made. Before doing this drill, I like to do some

small footwork drills working on faking one way, going the other (mini zigzags) and faking and then proceeding that way. I also encourage the contact lead here where the offensive player seeks slight contact with the defence before they lead.

Monkeys in the Middle
In this drill, the offence has a one player advantage over the defence and this can be 3 on 2, 4 on 3, 5 on 4 and requires the offence to make good decisions and the defence to anticipate, pressure and hustle.

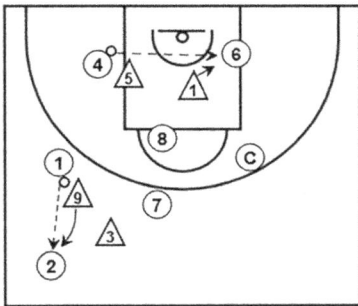

Diagram 3a) In this drill I have ten players split in to two teams of five with three offensive players with one ball forming a triangle at least three to four metres apart and two defensive players within the triangle. The offensive players try and make as many passes as possible which are determined by the coach or a time limit where the coach can then change some of the offence to the defensive team. Another way of rotating players is to have the defence steal the ball which can be the only way they get off defence.

Points of Emphasis

- Offensive players fake a pass make a pass and try not to telegraph where you are passing to so the non-pressuring defender can't steal the ball

- The pass receiving players should have knees slightly bent and hands in a ready to catch position at all time

- Defensive player must pressure quickly to tie up the player with the ball and make it harder for them to pass by mirroring the ball with active hands

Square Passing Drill
A simple pass and move drill that soon has the players under pressure as they need to concentrate and make decisions based on the whistle.

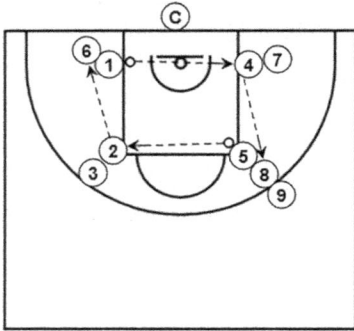

Diagram 4a) Set the players up in a square using the key as a good guide, or cones and flat discs which can also be used. With players evenly spread you can use one to four balls as the players advance their skills. Here players are using two balls, passing and following their pass which is rather simple until the coach blows the whistle and then the balls must be passed in the opposite direction and if you passed the ball you must follow the pass to the other line. This drill gets more complicated the more balls that are in the drill. The final variation that really has the players thinking is pass and go in the opposite direction to the pass. I hold off on this variation until players have advanced their skills and understanding of the game.

BASIC DRIBBLING DRILLS

After demonstrating the dribble technique to the team it's time to get them working.

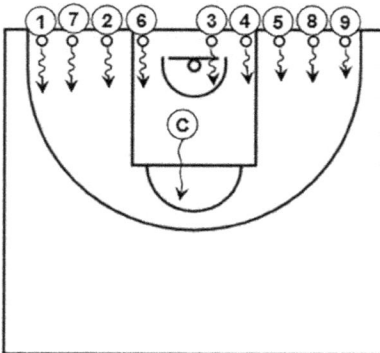

Diagram 1a) Have all the players line up on the baseline after reviewing dribbling technique, then have them work half or full court. Now it is most important that players dribble with their eyes up, so here I have them look at me the coach and hold my hand up showing a number on my hand with my fingers and encourage all players to call out the number. As they move forward, I move back and change the number every few seconds and it really helps to have an assistant coach, manager, parent or older player at one end and you the coach at the other end. I also have players look at the roof while executing basic dribbles. Have the players change dribbling hands on returning back to the baseline.

Dribble Variations

- Stationary dribbles on both hands including crossovers and V dribbles

- Walking one step, one bounce moving up the court

- Control, hesitation, pullback, crossover and speed dribbling

- Hopping, jumping feet together and backwards to increase difficulty

- Dropping down on one knee or on your back while keeping the dribble going

- Dribbling with eyes closed to increase sensory touch and feel

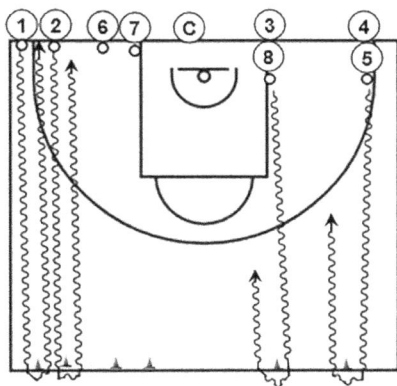

2a) Dribble Races

To add a little more competitiveness and excitement to training I add a racing element where two or more players compete.

Diagram 2a) Here cones are placed at the centre line but you can make it full court or even at the free throw line. The players must go around the cones which stops short cuts and adds an element of turning and negotiating an obstacle. The diagram shows two players against each other on one side of the court, but on the other side there are players working in teams, so this drill can be done many ways. I also run a handicap system that makes players chase a player which brings another level of competitiveness to training. You can add a small push-up penalty to increase the strength work for all the players, for losing players and teams if you need to help players get upper body strength.

Training Aids

Using props to assist play, the players development and also create obstacles that need to be negotiated on the court. This can be cones, chairs, bags, wheelie bins or props like cones, discs and D-Man that can be purchased via sport stores or online. I use them from time to time and they certainly simulate having a defender there. You can also use no peak dribble goggles for all and any drills and I saw a creative wheelchair basketball coach once placed 30 centimetre cardboard inserts attached to the front of the no peaks to make it even harder for players to look down while they were wheeling through a very tricky obstacle course.

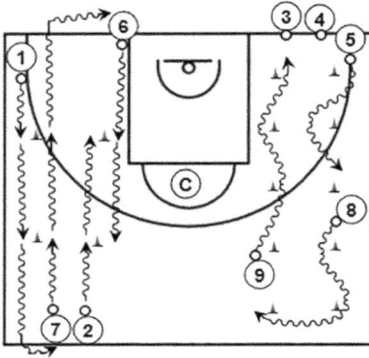

Diagram 3a) Here cones are used on both sides of the floor for the important practice of crossover and hesitation dribbling. So many players are reluctant to use their opposite hands during a game which really hampers their development, so drills like this at least compel them to use it. You can also make this competitive by setting up and racing using all the dribbles listed in the basic dribbling in **Diagram 1a)** on the previous page. Players after a while become a little bored and restless just doing these simple drills and tend to go through the motions. Adding a racing element and challenging tasks like hopping, jumping and moving backwards through the obstacles can keep players interest up as it is a change from normal movements.

Attack and Pull Back

Now young players have a tendency to stop when confronted by defensive players which allows even more pressure as it doesn't usually stop at one but multiple players heading towards the ball.

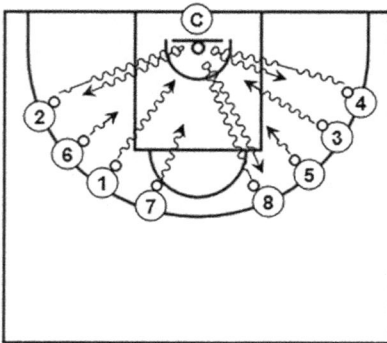

Diagram 4a) An easy set-up for the players here where they gather on the three-point line with a ball each and then drive directly to the basket placing their foot under it then retreat backwards with the ball behind them eyes forward and a protection arm up. Once the players return to the three-point line they cross the ball over to their opposite hand and attack on that opposite hand. The fact that multiple players

are converging on the same spot creates a lot of traffic at the point of the attack, so there will be a little contact when players get near the basket, which is valuable for practice and adds an element of pressure to the drill.

Multiple Player Dribble Drills
Dribble Knockout

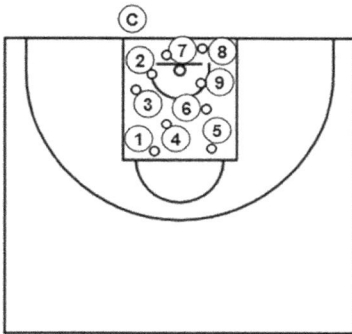

Diagram 1a) Every player has a ball and starts in the key or within the three-point line and it is important that you have a court where you can continually cut down the area as the number of players is reduced. On the whistle or the call of "**GO**" players start dribbling and attempt to knock their teammate's basketball out of the key or designated area, while maintaining legal control on the ball.

Rules

• Once your ball, not your body, is knocked out of the court, you're out

• If you double dribble, you're out

• If you carry the ball, you're out

• If you're too slow to move into the next area, you're out

• If you're not active in the game trying to knock the ball away, you're out

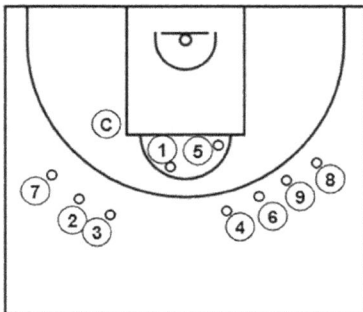

It is a great opportunity for coaches to really teach the double dribble and carry rule along with changing the drill up to only dribble on the off-hand.

Diagram 1b) As the players are knocked out, they move away from the area and I encourage them to either keep dribbling with their off-hand or do crossovers while they wait for the next game. Once you get down to the last two to four players move into the smallest area to finish the game.

Points of Emphasis
* Keep your eyes up and keep the ball low

* Be aggressive and attack other players trying to knock their ball away

* As much as possible protect the ball by keeping it close to the body

* React quickly to changes in moving to the smaller court area

* Create some contact to help players to get used to this aspect of the game

Face Off
A great drill that helps players keep their heads up and utilises various dribbles and you can also create some contact with the players.

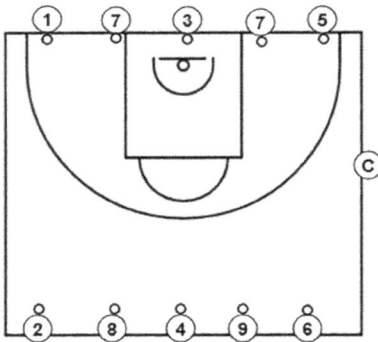

Diagram 2a) Players pair up and face each other with a ball each on the baseline and centre line. It is important to start this drill slowly as players may have challenges keeping their eyes up while dribbling and charging forward too fast may result in some needless bumps and knocks. It is important to develop various types of dribbles and the following should be a standard.

Basic Dribbles – These are a must

* **Hesitation** (Stop and Go) – two to three bounces keep it low then take a big first step and make sure the ball is protected

* **Crossover** – Players drive hard and crossover at the midpoint and the players crossing close to each other changing hands and coming back the opposite way on this hand.

* **Pull Back** – With this dribble the player pulls back two to three dribbles with a protection arm up and can either crossover or continue on with the strong hand.

- **Double Crossover** – Same as the crossover only the players cross the ball back to the same hand they started dribbling with and continue in that direction.

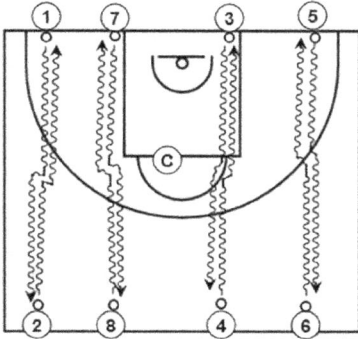

Diagram 2b) Players drive the ball at each other to a mid-point and then execute various dribbles then move past each other to the opposite line and change hands on the return journey. Ask for more speed as players gain more skills.

Advanced Dribbles – to challenge you players as they gain experience

- **Crossover Between the Legs** – Make sure the ball is positioned on the side of the body for the crossover which makes it easier to execute

- **Crossover Behind the Back** – Make sure the ball is back behind the body allowing it to be snapped behind and forward

- **Inside Out** – This is a fake crossover dribble bringing the ball to the opposite hip keeping the hand on top of the ball bring it back to the same side

- **Spin** – The spin dribble must be pulled back with the same hand to the opposite side of the body on a backward spin then picked up with the other hand

- **Fake Spin** – As the name implies you fake by turning back to spin then go back in the same direction using a quick crossover to sell the fake

Shark
Kids always love to play tagging games so anytime you can inject these into training sessions it will increase the fun and competitive nature of the players. Shark is a great game that will teach players not only to dribble under pressure with head and eyes up, but it will also help them think while on the move.

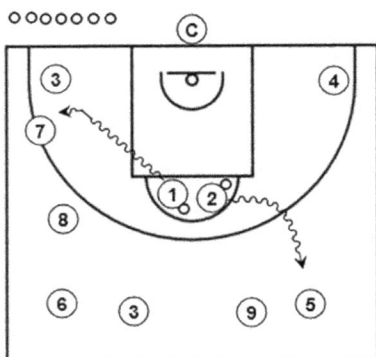

Diagram 3a) The Shark setup is quick and easy everyone has a ball but only two players will start with one in their hands. They are the Shark (here they start in the circle at the top of the key), the rest place their ball against the back or side wall and spread out on the court.

Diagram 3b) I tell the players the Shark is hungry and every time it tags you it grows bigger and once a player with a ball tags you, you're now on its team and you must race and grab a ball and attempt to tag the rest of the players. Last player to be tagged is the winner.

Variations

• Use the off-hand only

• Reduce or expand the size of the court depending on your numbers

Points of Emphasis

• All the usual things associated with dribbling – heads up – strong dribble – suction cup with the hand – snap the wrist – use both hands

• Encourage the Sharks to hunt in packs and corner players in the corner to make it easier to tag them

There are a few more drills that you can use to promote more dribbling in the FUN Drills section in a last part of this Chapter.

SHOOTING DRILLS

Shooting will be secondary to actually getting the ball down the floor so you can actually shoot it but once this is happening then you will want to spend a great deal of time on it. Technique **(covered in Chapter 2)** is the highest priority for any player, and then comes the need to have drills at training that help the team during games. As the game itself is dynamic in nature with built-in competitiveness and pressure, a coach should build this into their training sessions. I like to build competitive shooting drills into training and build an element of pressure that players will face in the game. We also have warm up shooting drills that can be used for games and as a lead up to the competitive drills which put players under pressure to score. The most important Point of Emphasis is shooting technique in combination with footwork in all drills and I like to do a high intensity drill and follow it with a low-intensity drill similar to the flow in a game.

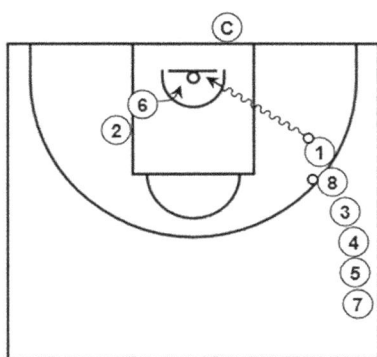

Diagram 1a) Two Line Layup Drill – This drill is a universal one that is used by virtually every team in the world as a simple warm up drill before a game. The setup is easy with one line starting at or just outside the three-point line or even the halfway line and the rebounding line on the opposite side to the basket either close or further out depending on the age and experience of the players. A minimum of two balls is good as it keeps the drill moving and more players are involved and after a while it should have a really good flow to it. The first player in the shooting line **(1)** drives the ball to the basket and shoots a layup, player **(6)** in the opposite line rebounds the ball.

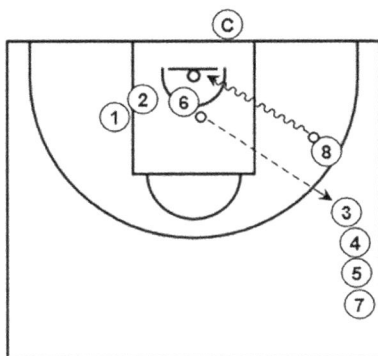

Diagram 1b) Once **(6)** secures the rebound they pass it to the next player in the shooting line **(3)** meanwhile **(8)** drives in for the next layup while **(1)** who shot the previous shot goes to the back of the rebounding line.

Points of Emphasis

- Drive hard heads up

- Shoot on a 45degree angle high and soft off the backboard

- Rebound strong above your head, pass strong to the shooting line

- Move to receive the pass, don't wait for the ball to come to you

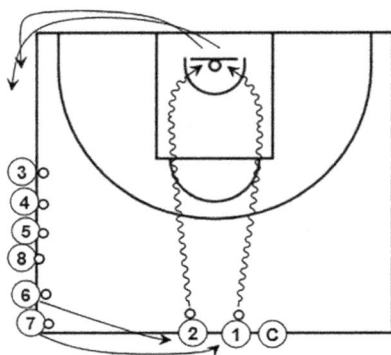

Layup Races

I like to put as many pressure situations as I can in our training as I find when nothing is on the line players can just go through the motions and lose focus and concentration. With layup races, there are strong drives to the basket and competition to beat their teammate to the score first. You can introduce multiple types of dribbling and shots, add more players and if you have a full court, players can work in both directions.

Diagram 2a) Before starting the drill the coach needs to match up the players in even pairs that give both players a chance to win the race. Once the pairs are sorted out have them line up on the sideline or in their pairs either side of the centre line with a ball each. The first pair **(1)** and **(2)** move into the centre circle and drive hard to the basket, first player to score wins. This is a great drill that lends itself to many variations.

- Shoot strong or off-hand layups

- Add various dribbles hesitation, crossovers, pull back and the score doesn't count unless you execute the dribble

- Shots from the block or free throw line, follow up with a rebound and shot

- Players can also throw the ball off the backboard on a rebound then shoot

- Limit shots to a maximum of three and if neither player scores a five-push-up penalty but if one player scores first within the three shots, three push-ups to the losing player

Spot Shooting

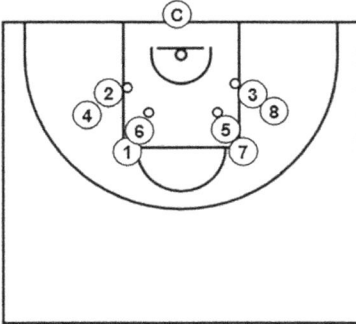

Diagram 3a) Here you have the opportunity to work on shooting technique close to the basket and then gradually increase the distance to at least the free throw line as players will need to do this if fouled in the act of shooting. I usually make this competitive first to three or five baskets then rotate a position. The losing teams can do a three or five push-up penalty to create a little pressure on the players and I find it makes them focus more when somethings on the line. You can also have players rebound and count the score as an extra which encourages following the shot and shooting again,

Three- line Shooting
Keeping with the high intensity, low intensity drills sequence at training, the next two drills complement each other and you can use cones, bags or chairs as a defensive player.

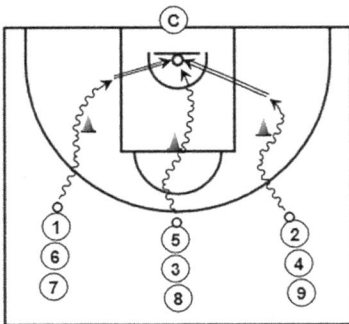

Diagram 4a) Here we have set-up cones in the middle of the free throw line and out left and right sides about free throw distance from the basket. Form three lines behind the three-point line, each line with a ball for the first player or alternately, every player could have one. The drill starts with the players driving and attacking the chair and once they pass it creating various shots. The coach has the option of giving the players one or more shots to create a score and build some rebounding into the drill. Make sure players use both hands on the drive and practice hesitations (stop and go), cross overs, double crossovers and pullback protection dribbles. The shots can be short or mid-range and add some rebounding and second shot attempts also coach.

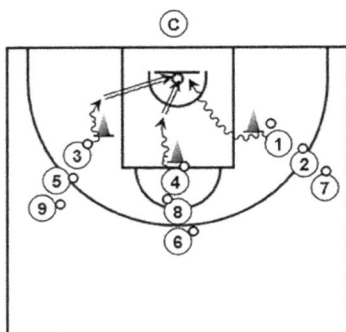

Diagram 5a) I like this option of three lines bringing players directly up to the cones and it is here we practice the basic three fakes (**shot, pass and dribble fake**) focussing on a big first step around the cone after the fake to give you an advantage over the defence in a real game situation. Now you can have all three lines doing the same fake and step around move or have each line represent one of the three fakes. It is important to practice the fakes and moves on both sides of the body.

Points of Emphasis

- Sell the fake (check out Chapter 2 on fakes) not too fast or slow convince the defence

- Dribble on the hand away from the defence

- Keep the pivot foot down on the bounce to avoid the travelling violation

- Step long and quick after the fake get head and shoulders in front of the defence

- Move fast after the fake but never rush the shot

Two Ball Knockout

This is a fun shooting drill that players absolutely love, is competitive and builds real pressure as the game reaches its conclusion.

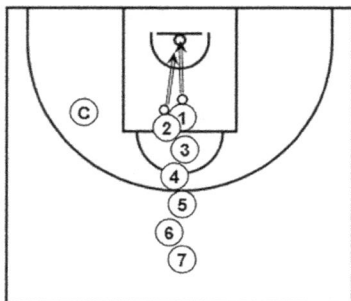

Diagram 6a) Players form a line that the coach feels is a good distance shot for the majority of shooters for their first shot. The first two players in line start with the balls and first in line shoots then the second player shoots trying to score before the first shooter and that is the basic main rule. If you score before the player in front of you,

they're out and if you score before the player behind you pass the ball back quickly so the next player in line has a chance to knock the player out in front of them. When you get down to the last two players you can end it two ways.

1) Let the players continue until a winner emerges.

2) Place the balls equal distance from the basket and the first to score a basket or two baskets win. You can also add a small task when the balls are equal distance for the final shootout. You do things like jumping jacks sprint to the halfway line and you can add a little fun to the finish, so be creative.

Change up the distances and angles where the players start from and you can also create a full court drill of continuous knockout where by once a player is knocked out, they stay in the contest and head down to the other end doing a small push-up penalty in the centre circle. The player with the least number of knockouts wins.

Pressure Spot Shooting

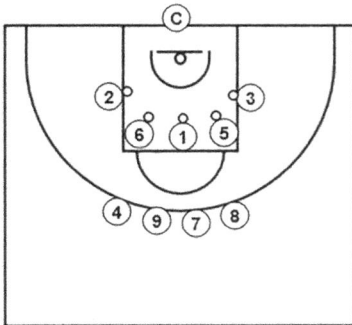

Diagram 7a) A simple set-up and this drill is perfect when you have an odd number of players. Players must shoot from the same spot each time and it's first to three or five baskets. The winner stays in the drill and must change the spot they start on for the next game as the losing players rotate out and the players at the three-point line rotate in. The winner also gets to say go for the next round and the losing players from the previous contest can do a small push-up or sit up penalty or, if everyone has a ball, have the players do some stationary dribbling drills. I start players close to the basket and eventually move them out to free throw distance. You can also add a dribble option from the three-point line.

BOARDS and Shoot
A great drill for both rebounding and shots off the rebound, this also gives the coach an opportunity to focus on a **Key Word** for rebounding **BOARDS.**

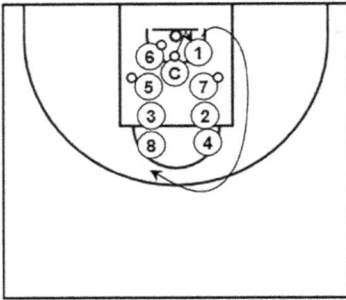

Diagram 8a) Coach stands in front of the basket and the players form 2 lines either side with a minimum of two balls but the more the better. Just before we start the drill I as the coach have everyone place the ball on the floor away from the players and have them focus on the rebounding technique (**see chapter 2**). After many repetitions of technique practice and the coach calling out **BOARDS,** we are ready to start the drill. Player **(1)** hands the ball to the coach who throws the ball up on the board and then they rebound above their heads and then shoot using the backboard. Once the player finishes the shot they head back around the drill and change lines to practice on both sides of the basket. The coach then alternates, throwing the ball up on both sides of the basket. I prefer this to the players throwing it up themselves, as it gets them to watch the ball out of the hand and then get after it as they would in a real game.

BOARDS Shot Outlet Layup Full Court

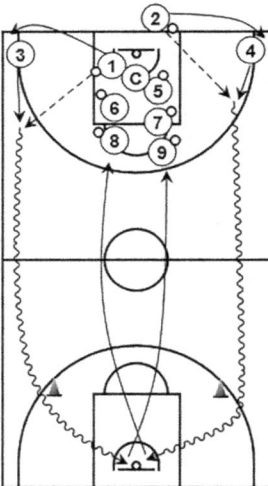

Diagram 9a) This drill follows on from **BOARDS** and shoot, except we add an outlet player **(3)** and **(4)** on the left and right side-lines starting near the baseline. In this diagram, the coach only allows one shot so if it goes in, the players must take it out over the baseline. Player **(2)** has made the basket so they take the ball out, which simulates an opponent who has made a basket, then they make an outlet pass to **(4)** who pushes forward to receive the ball and drives down for a full court layup, rebounds their own shot and comes back and changes lines. Meanwhile the other side **(1)** missed the shot so they act as if they have just taken a defensive rebound and make an outlet pass to **(3)** breaking down the court again for a full court layup, then comes back to the opposite line. Then **(2)** and **(1)** replace **(3)** and **(4)** in the rotation to be the next receivers when **(6)** and **(5)** take their turns rebounding and shooting. There are many

modifications and variations you can make to this and many of the drills listed. Different types of dribbles, passes, fakes and shots can help players adjust to what they will face or do in a game.

COMBINATION DRILLS

I love combination drills as they really help players accelerate their skills and by using multiple skills, can simulate a game situation which is important. It can also free up training time to work on other important components that will help you build your teams skills on both ends of the floor.

Baseline Dribble, Pivot, Pass
A good starting multiskill drill that's easy to set-up where players can quickly execute four to five skills in really quick time.

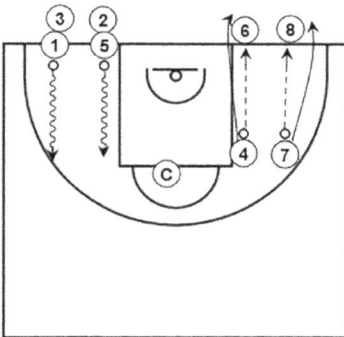

Diagram 1a) Players pair up on the baseline with a ball with the player with the ball in front. From this starting position, they then drive to the free throw line or a slightly less distance for really younger players and jump stop, pivot 180 degrees, make a pass back to their teammate, then go back to the starting point to allow their teammate to then drive to the free throw line and so the drill continues. It is also quick to add changes to the dribble **(right/left hand, hesitations, crossovers, drop down on one knee and protection dribble)** and passes **(chest, bounce, overhead, side step one handed bounce pass)** along with adding some **pass and dribble fakes**.

Side-line Dribble, Pass, Lead
Following on from the previous drill this one adds more dribbling and leading rather than receiving the ball in a stationary position.

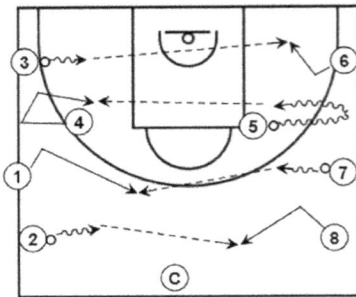

Diagram 2a) Players pair up and start on opposite sidelines with one ball per pair. The drill starts with a drive towards their teammate who makes eye contact and then executes a **SLOW ZIG – FAST ZAG** lead with a target hand. After catching the ball, the player then pivots back towards the baseline and drives to the side-line then turns back looking for their teammate who after the pass also heads back to the sideline to set-up the next lead. The two main points of emphasis here

- Dribble with the eyes up and pass strong to the leading hand without travelling

- See the ball into the hand on the catch and establish a pivot foot without travelling (not easy for a beginner but well worth the effort)

Pass Exchange Drive and Score
A good drill that has all the players and the coach actively involved throughout the drill although after a while you can have the players take the lead role out the front.

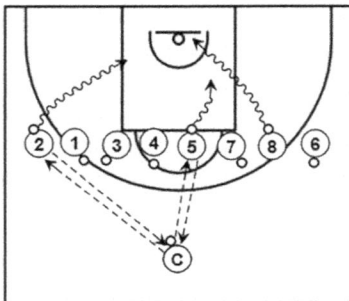

Diagram 3a) Every player and the coach have a ball each and the coach stands out in front of a line of players who're standing above the free throw line or a little further out if the players are older. The drill starts with every player and the coach dribbling the ball on the spot, the players focussing their attention on the coach who'll be throwing a bounce pass directly to a player who must then return their ball via a chest pass to the coach. Once the basketballs have been exchanged, the player turns towards the basket and drives hard to shoot. The coach makes their way down the line making sure all the players are one, looking at them and two, are all involved in passing, driving and shooting. This drill lends itself to multiple types of dribbles, follow up rebounds and shots. The pass exchange

makes players react quickly which then transfers to the dribble, but not the shot which should never be rushed.

Two-line Multiskill Layup Drill
Another great multiskill drill combining every offensive skill needed for a beginner player and one in which a coach can modify and add various dribbles, passes, shots and rebounds.

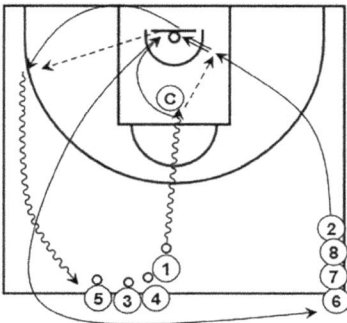

Diagram 4a) One line with balls starting at the centre circle and a shooting line towards the side-line, with the coach lining up just under the free throw line simulating a defender. Player **(1)** drives hard at the coach while **(2)** runs the lane then cuts to the basket to receive the bounce pass for the layup then after the shot continues through to the opposite wing. After **(1)** makes the pass they rebound the ball and make an outlet pass back to **(2)** who dribbles to the centre line and **(1)** makes their way to the shooting line by going around the line at the circle, not cutting through the middle. If the ball goes in the basket, the rebounding player can take it over the baseline to make the outlet pass simulating what they would do in an actual game if an opposition player made the basket. Coaches, get creative here and change up the dribbles, the passes and make sure the drill switches sides, giving equal time on both sides of the floor.

Two-man Half-court Series
This is one of the drills we use quite a lot at many of our training sessions and lends itself well to large and small teams and squads where you can have two or more players in each line but the majority of the drills involve only two players and I like to keep adding more components as the players get more experience. With beginners, it is always important to go over basic technique of dribbling, passing, catching, shooting and rebounding and get all players to simulate without the ball. This will eventually plant the seeds to help players develop quickly more so than if these important details were overlooked.

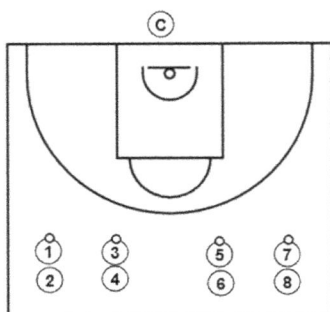

Diagram 5a) The setup is very easy with players spread evenly in a minimum of two players plus and a ball for each line. The coach should set themselves up behind the basket for the initial drill and then roam among the players to stop them and make corrections.

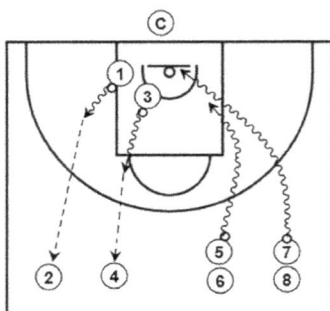

Diagram 5b) Here the players drive to the basket, shoot the ball, rebound dribble back out and pass to a teammate and it is always a good idea to play to a set number of baskets to give players a sense of urgency and something to play for rather than going through the motions and include a small push-up penalty for losing teams to provide some vital strength work.

Points of Emphasis and Variations

• Big first step on the drive (bounce the ball before lifting the pivot foot) with eyes up slow down on the last step for a steady layup

• See the ball into the hands on the catch and the two-handed rebound

• Dribbles – control, hesitation, crossover, pullbacks

• Use cones, discs, chairs and bags and place these in line with each team to act as a defender for them to practice dribble moves on

• Shots – layups, set shots, overhead shots

• Passes – chest, bounce, hand offs

• Add mini **ZIGZAGS** rather than stand and wait for the ball

Two Player Options
I like the two player options as it promotes teamwork and allows you to add a live defender to simulate real game situations.

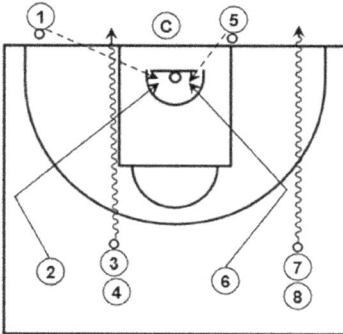

Diagram 5c) Here the player with the ball drives the ball to the baseline making sure they are at least two steps back from the line, then turn and face their teammates ready to pass the ball. The player without the ball now makes a **SLOW ZIG FAST ZAG** with a target hand cut to the basket for a catch and shoot or catch and bounce then shoot option. You can also have players move up to the three-point line to practice our out of bounds play **SNAKES** and the cuts which players can move and practice from the three angles. All the usual points of emphasis apply and coaches can change up passes and shots.

Adding Defensive Options

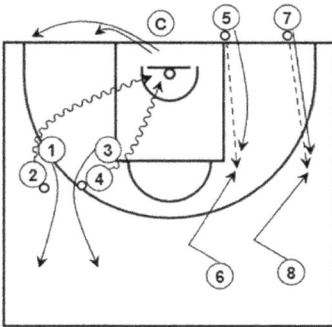

Diagram 5d) Using the set-up from the previous drill where there is a player ready to pass on the baseline and one cutting, have the player with the ball pass early rather than when the cutter is close to the basket. Here **(6)** and **(8)** are leading and receiving passes from **(5)** and **(7)** who then close out and pressure, trying to bat the ball away or rip it out of their hands for five to ten seconds. The offensive players can only pivot and protect the ball without dribbling during this time and I encourage the defender to be a little physical with some contact to get players used to this while still protecting the ball, as not all contact in games will be judged as fouls. On the opposite side **(2)** and **(4)** have been protecting the ball for the allotted time and now fake and drive to the basket while **(1)** and **(3)** move to the starting positions for the next leads. After shooting their shot **(2)** and **(4)** take positions on the baseline ready to pass to the leading **(1)** and **(3)** and the drill continues. After the

pivoting and protecting drill I like to put in a protection dribble drill which is the same as the previous one except players dribble for 10–20 bounces on each hand in a stationary position while the defence is trying to steal the ball from them. The coach can choose what options take place after this in regards to shots, but the rotation is the same as players switch positions. Encourage the defensive players to be aggressive to help their teammates adjust to this type of pressure.

Quick Pass Lead and Shoot
A great drill which gets a lot of passes, footwork and shots up in a short period of time.

Diagram 6a), 6b) & 6c) Place two players at the elbows **(4)** and **(5)** who become the passers, with all other players with a ball on the baseline forming two lines on the edge of the key **(8)** and **(3)** who are first in line make the first pass to the elbows. After passing, they make a zigzag cut stepping towards the basket then out to the wing looking to receive the pass back from **(4)** and **(5)** and from this position they can shoot an outside shot or drive to the basket. After shooting the shot that was determined by the coach, players **(8)** and **(3)** rotate to opposite sides and the next two players **(1)** and **(6)** continue the drill making the next pass to the elbows. After every minute, change the passers at the elbows so all players get an equal time to pass lead and shoot.

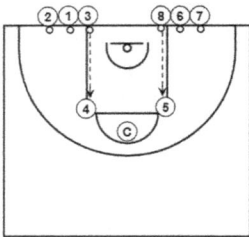

6a) Set-Up	6b) Pass and Lead	6c) Rotation

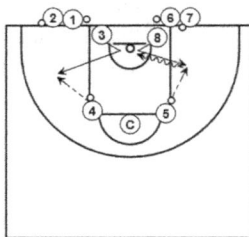

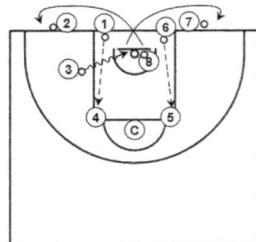

Diagram 6d) Variation 1 – cones are placed out wide on the wings but within the three-point line and players after passing, lead out past the cones with an outside target hand, then cut back hard to the basket for a pass and shoot, or pass, drive and shot options.

Diagram 6e) Variation 2 – cones are placed outside the key and here players catch and shoot over the cones, then follow the shot to rebound and take a follow up shot.

Diagram 6f) Variation 3 – follows on from the previous drill except this time players must fake first before a quick dribble move around the cone and can drive all the way to the basket or pull up for a shot just past the cone.

6d) Variation 1	**6e) Variation 2**	**6f) Variation 3**

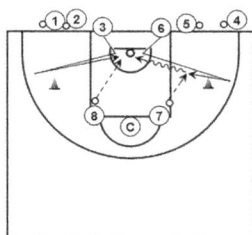

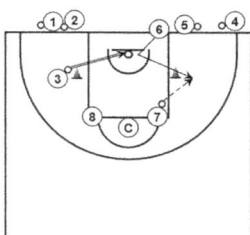

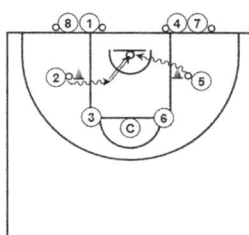

Full Court Layup Drill

A great drill if you have a full court to train on, as it lends itself to many offensive skills and you can also add individual defence.

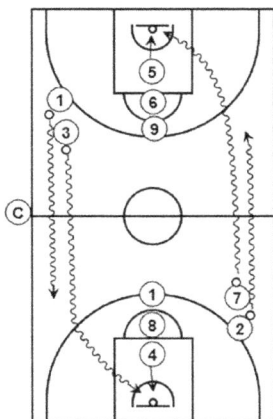

Diagram 7a) The setup is quick and easy and works better with larger teams or a combination of teams. You start with two to four players with basketballs on one of the wings at each end, facing down the court and the players without the ball line up on opposite ends in a line facing the basket which forms the rebounding line. Coach starts the drill calling out **GO** to the first player on each wing (who then drive to the basket for a layup) and after they've taken several dribbles the coach then calls next player **GO,** they also drive to the basket for the layup.

Diagram 7b) After shooting their layups the players then return to the end they have come from, moving to the back of the rebounding line. The front player in the rebounding line rebounds the shot, then drives down the floor to shoot their layup before coming back to the same end they rebounded from. After a few minutes the drill changes side for valuable opposite hand practice. Now the coach can add all types of dribbles here and I add hesitations at the three point lines and the centre line as well as crossovers, pullbacks and speed dribbles. Players can shoot layups, set shots or overhead shots and the coach can make it a set time or a number of made baskets. As players get more experience you can add a small push-up penalty for missing layups and/or dribbling with their heads down to increase their focus on simple tasks but with beginners even though we build strength work into the program it shouldn't be for missing shots early in their basketball careers.

Diagram 7c) Here we add a defensive component to the drill by having the rebounders **(4)** and **(5)** take the ball to the baseline, in this case the right-hand side of the floor and the player who shot the ball **(3)** and **(7)** instead of running back to the other end, now plays defence on the dribbler until the centre line, then drops off and returns to the rebounding line. With the first phase of defensive plays, I have players keep their hands on their shorts working on footwork and position which also allows the offensive players to dribble the ball without having it stolen. In the second phase, the defence keeps their hands out to the side for better balance, again concentrating on their footwork and position. In the third phase, we allow the defence to steal the ball but they must maintain good position and give the ball back if they steal it until both players hit the centre line. The points of emphasis for the offensive players are simple-protect the ball with the body, bounce strong and keep the head up and eyes forward with hesitations, sharp crossovers and if they get ahead of the defence, to stop and let the defender re-establish position.

FAST BREAK ADVANTAGE DRILLS

Young players especially beginners in their first few games, may really struggle with getting shots up and even scoring a basket. This can be a little deflating for the kids so at training I like to help them have a little success in a game situation. Initially we start with advantage drills in the quarter-court and then advance to fast break drills at the half and full court which opens up great opportunities when used in tandem with the **SPLIT**. We do this with both two on one and three on two drills especially for beginners, to create the extra player and give players an opportunity to score without the pressure of a five on five game.

Two on One Quarter-court

Diagram 1a) & 1b) Coach starts with the ball and the offensive players form two lines outside the three-point line left and right of the basket. The defensive player **(3)** starts in the middle of the key and another **(6)** ready to rotate in next play. The coach makes the first pass to one of the offensive lines and encourages the front two players to move forward and attack the basket. At the completion of the play the last player to shoot or touch the ball rotates to the back, the player waiting behind the baseline rotates in. The defensive player (3) and the non-shooter (4) move off to the side of the court and back to the offensive lines.

1a) Set-Up   **1b) Rotation**

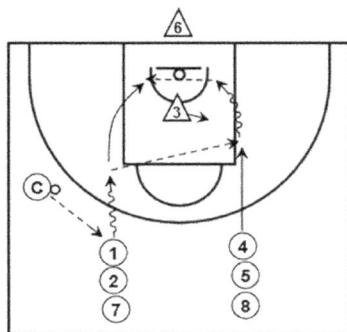 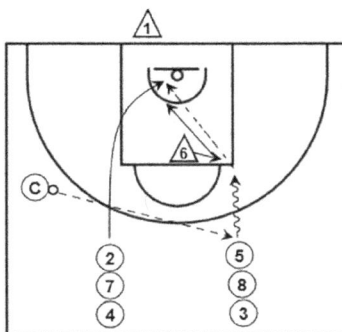

Points of Emphasis

- Stop the drill when players are running with the ball and double dribbling and explain and make corrections and allow the players to continue the drill

- Use Key words **DRIVE – NEXT PASS – PRESSURE THE BALL – SMOTHER**

- Drive with heads up and draw the defence then pass

- Look after the ball

- Players without the ball cut toward the basket and get ahead of the ball

- All players rebound – **BOARDS**

- Shoot good shots

Three on Two Quarter-court

The next step after the two on one is three on two which is building more opportunities for players to get shots in a controlled drill. Here the coach can be close to the action and give great feedback to the players without the background noise of the game, where communication can sometimes be very difficult. Now we also start introducing really good defensive concepts and Key Words that help players learn these. Coach, the Key Word system will really accelerate the players and teams progress.

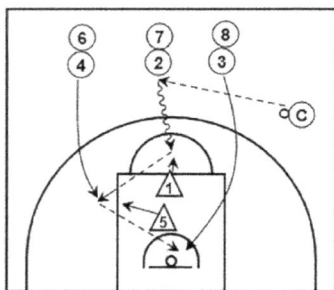

Diagram 2a) Coach starts with the ball and positions themselves on the side of the drill between the offense and defense. The offense forms three lines outside the three-point line spread evenly across the court. The defense starts in the key in a one up one back position. The drill starts when the coach passes the ball to one of the offensive lines and all players move forward attacking the defense.

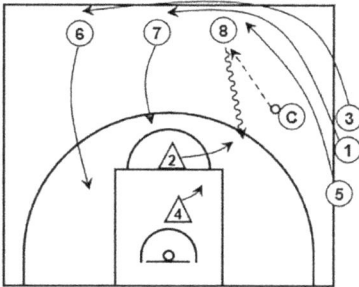

Diagram 2b) At the end of the play the last player on offense to touch the ball rotates out to the side with the two defensive players and then back to the offensive lines. The two players on offense that didn't touch the ball last stay as the next two defenders. At the end of the play the ball is passed back to the coach who makes sure it is safe to start the next play and also a great chance to give feedback to the players in between plays.

Points of Emphasis

All the same points that applied to two on one apply here also with a few additional ones which are mainly for the defensive players.

- Closest defender pressures the ball
- The player not pressuring the ball must protect the basket from the easy shot
- Encourage players to pass the ball before they are under pressure
- Fake a pass to make a pass
- Look towards the basket every time you have the ball
- **HUSTLE** with the feet
- Shoot good shots

Half-court Two on One Tap and Go

Once players have played a few games, I like to do drills that simulate what they tend to face in a real game. This drill now adds an element of surprise to it and we also start further out from the basket. There is still the advantage of the extra player on offence, but the defensive player gets to react as they would in a game, having to race back and establish position.

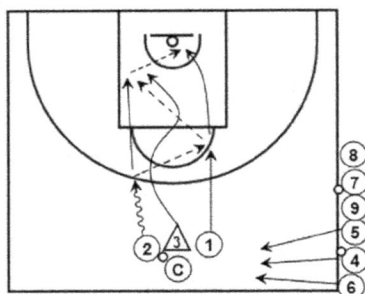

Diagram 3a) The coach takes a position in a centre circle and the players form a line on the side-line with a ball for every three players in line. The first three players pass the ball to the coach and then get in a huddle close enough so the coach can tap a player and hand the ball off to another. Here the coach has tapped player **(3)** who now becomes the defence and handed the ball to player **(2)** who can either drive or pass while player **(1)** breaks away on the **SPLIT** looking to beat the defender to the basket to create an easy shot. The very nature of quickly tapping one player handing the ball to another and calling out "GO" as in a race, creates a sense of urgency which adds another dynamic to the drill helping players learn to play and react faster.

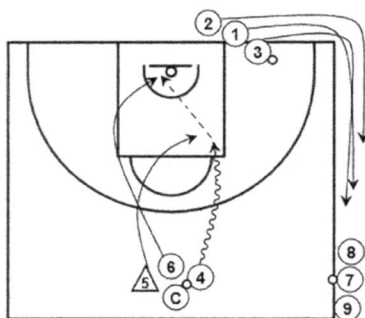

Diagram 3b) As soon as the first three players are on their way to the basket the next three players come out and the coach waits until the previous team finishes and move off the court via the base and side line rotating back to the middle. If you have an assistant coach then they can run the drill while you concentrate on the corrections and points of emphasis as well as a little bit of praise when players make a great pass or hustle on defence. If you have a full court you can send the next team to the opposite end which will have the players working hard and gaining more opportunity to practice.

All the same **Points of Emphasis** that applied to the quarter-court two on one definitely apply here, with importance given to the **SPLIT** and the defensive player getting **BACK** quickly. This is also a great way to build much needed game pressure on players while giving them a better chance to get shots up and enjoy this part of the game, especially if they're struggling during games.

Half Court Three on Two Tap and Go
This drill flows well from the half court two on one tap and go drill and the

players will have a far better idea of the workings of the drill and getting started. With more players, there will be more opportunity to give great feedback about the way they're working with their teammates along with their skills.

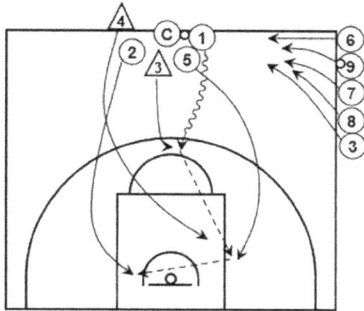

Diagram 4a) Coach starts in the centre circle with all the players on the sideline with one ball for every five players. The first five players run to the coach who's holding the ball in readiness for the drill. This time the coach needs to tap two players and, in this instance, **(3)** and **(4)** have been selected as the defence and **(1)** has been handed the ball with **(5)** and **(2)** joining **(1)** on offence. It now becomes a sprint to the basket and the coach will have their work cut out for them keeping up with the corrections and feedback for both offence and defence, but as the players gain experience it will flow and the decision making will get far better.

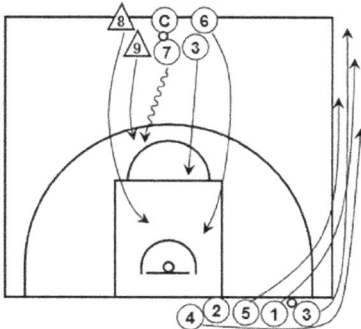

Diagram 4b) The coach must wait for the players to clear at the end of the play before letting the next eager group have their turn and if you have less than ten players you will need to wait for players to rotate out to join the next team. Make sure if you have ten or more players in the drill that players are not running back through the drill. If you have a full court then utilise both ends as it keeps more players working and gaining valuable experience.

The Points of Emphasis that applied to the quarter-court three on two definitely apply here along with a few extra points.

Offence – must balance the floor out to the centre, right and left lanes if they can't outrun and get in front of the defensive players. Stay in the **SPLIT** otherwise one defender can easily guard two players.

Defence – Try and force the offence into poor shots by defending closer to the basket. Pressure the ball as much as possible.

Everybody must rebound **BOARDS!**
Three-man Weave Two on One Full Court
The three-man weave is a very universal drill in the basketball world and is a great drill to teach young players how to pass and then get ahead of the ball. In this drill, we are also working on quick passing, quick footwork and just like the two on one tap drill simulates the game but with the added benefit of extra passing beforehand.

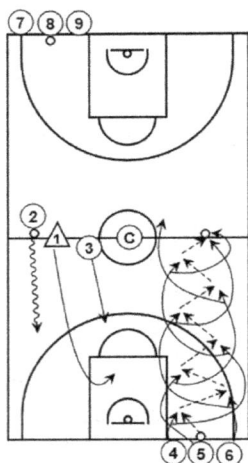

Diagram 5a) Have the players form three tight lines to the right or left side of the baseline and it is important that you practice this drill on both sides of the floor. The players run a tight three-man weave to the centre line and the first player in the weave to reach this line with the ball, must place it on the floor and then get back on defence. The other two players who are now on offence pick up the ball and attack the defensive player splitting left and right of the basket.

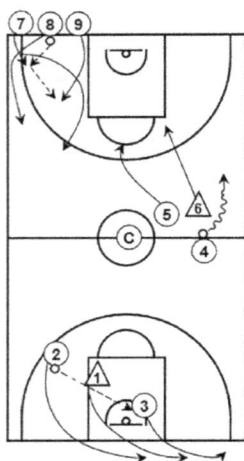

Diagram 5b) On completion of the play the players move to the back of the court and I tell the next team coming behind them to wait until the ball passes the three-point line for the team ahead of them before they start their weave. In the early training sessions, you may want the shot to go up before the next team starts their play.

With beginners, the coach will need to follow the teams to the centre line to make sure they are passing and running behind their teammates and getting ahead of the ball. You will also need to tell players to drop the ball and then encourage the offence to pick it up and move forward with a drive or pass and not run with the ball.

Points of Emphasis

- All the points in the previous drills apply

- Quick feet and hands and good passes on the weave

- Players who drop the ball get back quickly on defence and **SMOTHER** close to the basket

- Players who pick the ball up attack the basket with strong drives and smart passes

- All players rebound **BOARDS**

Five-man Weave Three-on-Two Full Court
As players become comfortable with the 3man weave you can now step it up to the five-man weave three on two drill. Depending on the size of the team or squad training at the session you can run the drill in a straight line just down the middle, or condense this off to the side of the court for a larger squad or if two or three teams are training together, which is what we do at our club.

Diagram 6a) If you're using the whole court, the setup is pretty easy with five players spread across the floor. The following is the condensed version **(1)** passes to **(3)** and runs behind both **(3)** and **(5)** and gets ahead of the ball which is the main objective of any weave drill. As the players get close to the centre line the same rule applies, which is the first player there drops the ball, but because it's a five-player drill and we need a second defender, the last player to pass to the player who drops the ball on the centre line becomes the defence as well. In this diagram (3) and (2) end up as the defenders, player (1) picks up the ball, (4) and (5) fill the right and left lanes to balance the floor, which is the best way to attack the defence.

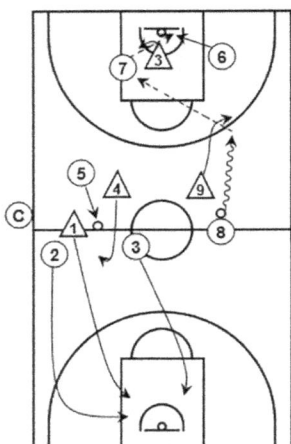

Diagram 6b) If you have a larger squad of players then running two teams from opposite ends will keep the players working rather than watching. It is important that the weave is really tight to the side-line and if there is space on the side of the court you can take the side-line out of it until the ball is dropped so the team coming the opposite way has space to execute the three on two.

Footwork, strong passing, **DRIVE** hard, defensive **COVER**, transition both ways, **SMOTHER**, **BOARDS**, fakes are all important points a coach needs to stay on top of.

Half-court Three-man Weave Two on One and Five-man Weave Three on Two
Not all teams have a full court to train on and many clubs run a half court one team training system. Keeping this in mind I think it's important to try and simulate full court training and conditioning work when you can. The three-man and five-man weave back two on one and three on two, are great drills to add multiskill elements and game play.

Diagram 7a) & 7b) This drill works really well with constant activity, with players shifting sides to utilise both left and the right side of the court. As soon as one team heads back on the 2 on 1, the next weave starts and you should ensure players rotate to opposite sides each time they finish a play.

7a) Set-Up   **7b) Rotations**

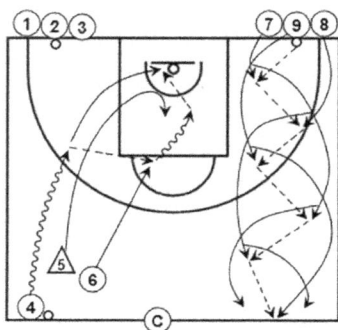 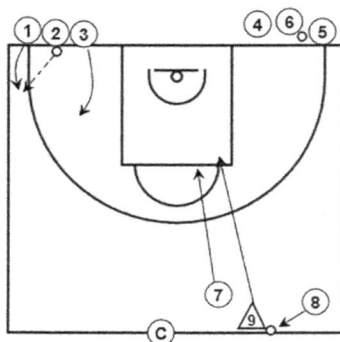

Diagram 8a) & 8b) Same setup as the full court drill with players turning back instead of continuing forward, which is a great drill where the coach can give great feedback on the weave and the three on two.

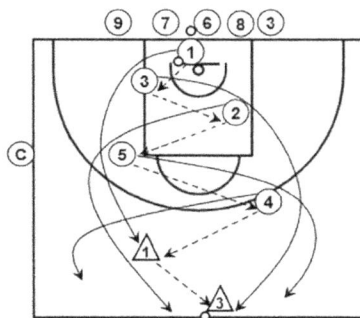

8a) Set-Up   **8b) Coach Gives plenty of Feedback**

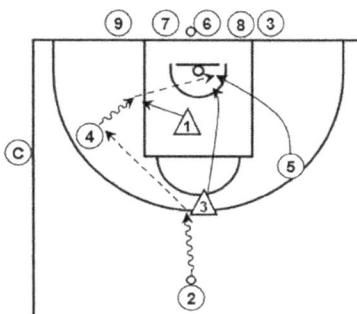

FUN DRILLS

News flash, coach, players play basketball to share good times with friends, stay healthy and most of all have fun. Training can be a grind at times and having a few drills on hand to change it up or end on a good note is always a great idea. I sometimes have a whole session of just fun drills, yet these drills are also designed to help improve footwork, balance, agility, strategy and concentration. All are valuable skills that compliment regular basketball training and are competitive and fun.

Fun Drills

• In Out

• Two-man Tag & Knee Boxing

• Thomas the Tank

• Chain Tag

• Octopus

• Shark

• Numbers

• Coach Says

• Tunnel Ball

In – Out
A great game that only needs a line, a little focus and concentration.

Diagram 1a) Players start behind the baseline and the coach explains the rules.

- Coach says **"IN"** you jump forward. If you jump back – you're OUT

- Coach says **"OUT"** you jump back. If you jump forward – you're OUT

- If your foot is touching the line – you're OUT

- Coach calls **"SPEED MODE"** last player across the line is OUT

Diagram 1b) The game continues to the last player who is declared the winner and if the last 2 or 3 go out at the same time then the coach wins. You can change the names you call "out" to colours or fruits, or have the players jump sideways, hop or stand in a defensive stance while jumping over.

1a) Set-Up   **1b) Rotation**

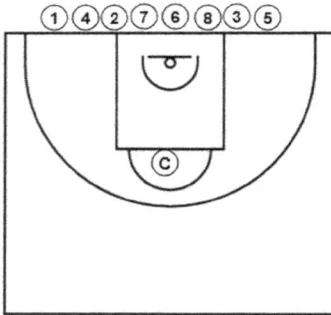
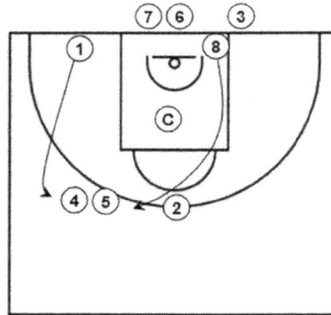

Two-man Tag
As a kid I loved playing tag, or we called it back then 'tiggy' and kids today are no different, yet you can turn a simple game into a useful warm up or fun drill that promotes quick reaction time and footwork.

Diagram 2a) & 2b) The setup – pair players up and have them spread out on the court and explain the rules.

- One player put your hand in the air – this is the first tagger

- Players must face each other at all times

- For safety reasons the tagger must stop and warn their teammate if they look like running into other players

Players go back and forth tagging each other for 15–20 seconds then the coach can call "'change'" so everyone swaps partners and the game continues. You may want to have the tagger count to two before they chase their teammate to give them a chance to put a little space between them and to use some footwork.

Knee Boxing

I follow two-man tag with knee boxing as tag will be majority offensive footwork and knee boxing really works the defensive side of the game.

Diagram 2a & 2b) Players pair up spread out on the court facing each other in a defensive stance and the coach explains the rules.

- Safety first, so make sure you keep your head centred between your feet allowing you to swing your arms, tapping the knee without losing balance and leading head first

- First player to three taps on both knees wins the game or after 20-30 seconds rotate the pairs

- Players must be active with feet and hands

This is a great reflex drill and one where you may need to encourage players to be active as they may stand off a little. Remember it is boxing so the idea here is to hit or tap and then not get hit in return.

2a) Set-up

2b) Rotation

Thomas the Tank

This is a great defensive footwork team drill that adds a little fun to training and yet is great practice for basketball as it becomes a team effort to win.

Diagram 3a) I start by telling the players about the caboose that was being left off the train by Thomas and the other carriages and they're in no hurry to let them back on.

- **(1)** and **(5)** are the Caboose

- (2) and (6) are Thomas the Tank Engine

- **(3), (4), (7)** and **(8)** are the carriages and must grip the player in front of them by having a strong grasp on their shirt as this creates the train

Diagram 3b) The rules of the game are simple, the Caboose is trying to attach itself to the train and the coach gives them 10, 15 to 20 seconds to complete the task. The train use defensive footwork, especially Thomas at the front of the train, positioning themselves between the Caboose and the last player attached to the train.

Rules

A small Penalty to the losers three to five push-ups

- If the Caboose attaches to the back within the time limit, it wins

- If the train breaks apart within the time limit, the Caboose wins

- If the Caboose fails to get on the back and the train stays intact, the Caboose loses

Everyone takes it in turns to be both Caboose, Thomas and the Carriages. You can also mix up the teams so everyone gets to play against each other.

3a) Set-Up

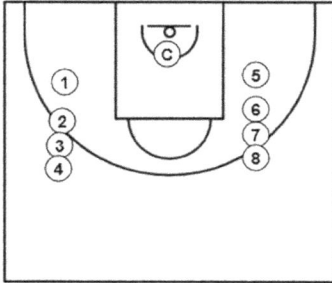

3b) 2 Ways to Win

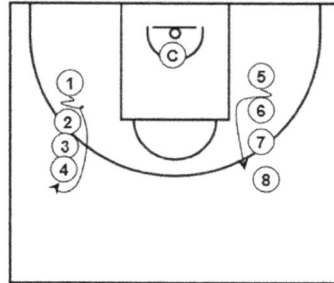

Chain Tag
Another tagging game kids love to play and this time it is played with small teams holding hands which adds a degree of difficulty and coordination to the game along with a lot of footwork as player dodge and weave to avoid being tagged.

Diagram 4a) Depending on the size of the squad or team of players this will determine the court size you use.

Full court 15+ players
Half-court 8 – 15 players
Three-point line – baseline less than eight players

Start with one or two pairs holding hands in a small chain in a semi-circle, either free throw line or centre circle and the rest of the players spread themselves out on the court. The taggers take off after the loose players trying to tag them and if they work together rather than on their own it makes the job of tagging easier as you herd players into the corners as shown in the next diagram.

Diagram 4b) As players get tagged the chain grows bigger to three then finally four players, once the team builds to four, the chain breaks and splits into two and the game then continues until the last player is tagged.

4a) Set-U   **4b) Tagging Strategy Herd and Tag**

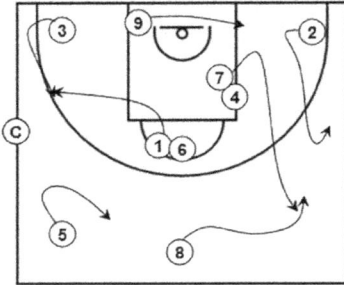

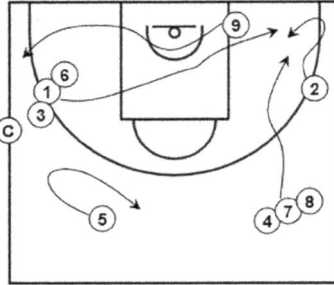

Octopus

This is a very popular tagging game at the club that our players love and one that has several variations so you can mix and add various skill elements to make it a little more challenging.

Diagram 5a) Divide the court into thirds either with cones discs or if netball lines are drawn on the court use those. Start with the taggers (**Octopus**) in the centre third of the court which is the only space they can operate in and tag. The rest of the team line up along the baseline and they have one simple task, to get to the other baseline without being tagged by an Octopus. They have five seconds to move into the middle third and they must stay within the side-lines.

Diagram 5b) If a player gets tagged by an Octopus, they become a seaweed and are basically standing in the spot and can tag but they can't move and chase. The game continues until all the players are tagged with the last player left declared the winner.

5a) Set-Up & Start   **5b) Second Run**

 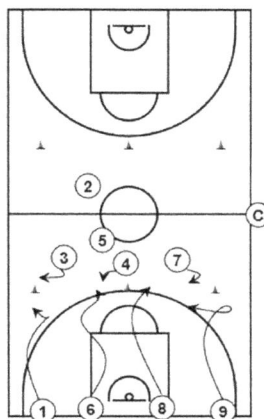

Variations

- Add a basketball for every player and turn it into an opportunity to improve dribbling skills with the footwork combined.

- Instead of seaweed who can tag, turn it into a scarecrow tiggy game where players can free up teammates by passing through their legs allowing them to continue to play

- Players can only hop, and must remain on that leg during their time in the tagging zone

- Players keep both feet together and jump while in the tagging zone

This game works well with larger squads of players or combining several teams.

Sharks

This game of Sharks is similar to Octopus with the same court set-up and taggers in the middle third that are the Sharks and are looking to increase their numbers.

Diagram 6a) & 6b) This game moves quite quickly as any player that starts on the baseline that is tagged becomes part of a school of moving sharks that unlike the seaweed Octopus, can move and tag more players. The rules are similar to Octopus though in that you only have five seconds to get into the middle third staying inside the side-lines and looking to get to the other baseline without being tagged. Last player tagged is the winner.

6a) Set-Up   6b) Building the Pool of Sharks

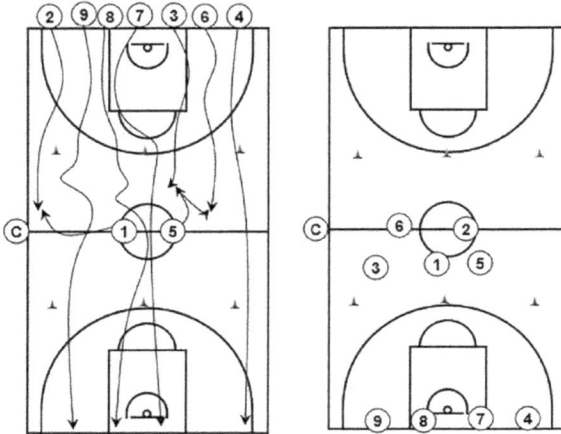

Variations

- Add a basketball for every player and turn it into an opportunity to improve dribbling skills with the footwork combined.
- Players can only use their off-hand to tag or dribble
- Players can only hop, and must remain on that leg during their time in the tagging zone
- Players keep both feet together and jump while in the tagging zone

This game works well when combining medium and larger squads of players.

Numbers
A really great game that players love and a fun drill I run occasionally, yet I have observed some coaches that run this at every single training session. I am huge on productive activity with players involved and working as much as possible yet the one on one component of this drill can leave players watching more than playing.

Diagram 7a) Pair players up in even match ups as in size, athleticism and skill level and each pair receives a number and heads to the opposite side-lines where they can stand, sit or lay on the floor. The coach stands in the middle of the court or even at the free throw line with a ball and simply calls out 1, 2, 3 or all 4 numbers and the players run out to get the ball and score a basket for their team.

Now in regards to the coach throwing the ball, they must make sure players are not heading directly at each other in a head on clash to get the ball. Safety of young players is paramount here, so wait until the player or players numbers you have called come out on the court and then have them jump up for the ball or scramble for it side by side. You can also shoot it at the basket and let the players fight for a rebound to start. If you only call one number and it takes a while for the players to score or even get a shot up, either stop the drill or call another number to join in and move the drill along. You can play to a time limit or a certain number of baskets. I like the contest to be as close and even as possible, so sometimes give the ball to the losing team at the time to allow them to get an easy first shot. If teams are uneven then balance them out coach, so it keeps the game interesting and nobody has to be too disappointed as it is meant to be a fun drill. I will often end the drill when scores are tied and tell the kids we can pick it up again at another session. Everyone shakes hands like we do after a game is finished.

7a) Set-Up Regular Game   **7b) Variation Shooting Game**

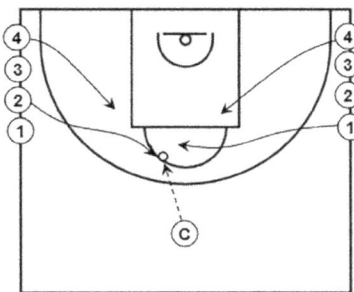

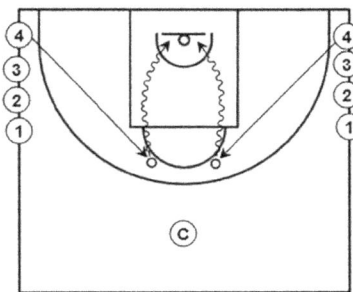

Diagram 7b) Here we turn the game into a competitive shooting game by adding another ball and placing them on the floor an even distance from the basket. The coach calls out 1 to 4 numbers and these players then try to score a

basket before the other player or players. Another variation is to have one player pass to all their teammates and then score placing the ball back on the place they picked it up from.

Coach Says

A great game to help players concentrate, working on many aspects of mainly defence in nature. It consists of several components that make it a challenging for younger and older players alike. As the name implies it is a basketball version of Simon Says which is replaced with **Coach Says**.

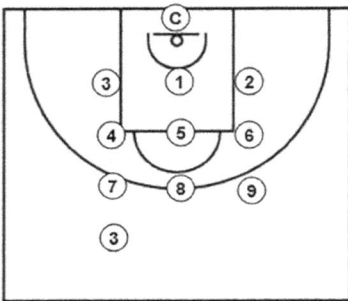

Diagram 8a) The coach stands on the middle of the baseline and the players form three, four or five lines depending on the number of players involved. They must be spread back at least three large steps to allow space to lie on the floor without touching the player in front or behind. Now the game has several components to it which the coach starts out both explaining, then having the players act out to have a full understanding of what is required of the skills involved.

Components

1. **Stance** – Coach yells **"STANCE"** and all the players jump out into a defensive stance and at the same time yell **"STANCE"**, repeat this several times

2. **Pitter Patter** – Coach yells **"PITTER PATTER"** once the players are in Stance and they move their feet quickly up and down on the spot, repeat several times

3. **Left** – The players are in a defensive stance and the Coach points with their right hand out to the side and yells **"LEFT"** the players then slide 3 times to their left yelling out **"LEFT, LEFT, LEFT"** repeat several times

4. **Right** – The players are in a defensive stance and the Coach points with their left hand out to the side and yells **"RIGHT"** the players then slide three times to their right yelling out **"RIGHT, RIGHT, RIGHT"**, repeat several times

5. **Rebound** – Coach yells **"REBOUND"** and the players jump in the air and clap above their head while yelling **"REBOUND"**, repeat several times

6. **Loose Ball** – Coach yells **"LOOSE BALL"** and the players hit the floor face down touching their chest to the floor then jumping back to their feet as quickly as possible, repeat several times and the last player up is out of the game

7. **Take the Charge** – Coach yells **"TAKE THE CHARGE"** and the players drop down on their backs touching their shoulder blades to the floor and then jump back up onto their feet as quickly as possible, repeat several times as the last player up is out of the game.

8. **Anything the coach says to get players out** – Coaches can get very creative in this endeavour, a little more on this in tricks on the next page.

Now that the players have learnt the components you are ready to play the game.

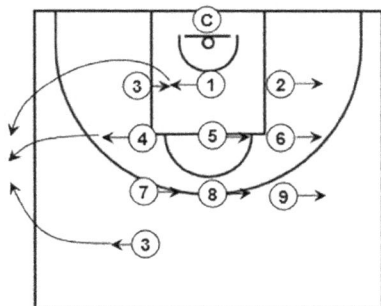

Diagram 8b) The coach must explain that the two words you must hear before you do anything is **"Coach Says"** – if this doesn't precede any command and you react, you're out. I usually give the players a chance if they go out on the very first command and I often go through the seven components in sequence making sure the players understand what they need to do before I really get into the game and getting players out. After a while, players get really good at the game and even the loose ball and take the charge calls can have players evenly matched in speed at hitting the floor and getting back up, although if you say these two commands enough you will eventually get one of the players out. If the group is large however this could take a while, so I add in the following to help coaches progress the game so players who are out early don't get too restless waiting for the last player to finish.

Coaches tricks to get players out

- Just yell **"STOP"** at any time the sheer shock value of this word will get a few players out, but this will only work for a certain time

- Asking player to move a little or reset the game also works but again only for a short time as players adjust

- Point in a different direction on the Left and Right call will work until players adjust

- On the Rebound call, I ask players to double clap, triple clap and doing this quickly also works well

- What's your name again? If they answer they're out

I am sure as a creative coach you will work out ways to move the game to quicker conclusions. I like to keep everyone interested and games that go on for extended minutes are not great for kids who get knocked out early. I even use speed mode here where last player to execute is out, as competitive kids will need to be challenged.

Tunnel Ball
An excellent game that I use to finish a basketball camp, which combines driving, shooting within teams and kids can call their team a fun name and chant this while they are playing. If you have a few coaches or older kids helping tout the team, they can also join in.

Diagram 9a) The setup is the same as traditional tunnel ball where players form lines outside the three-point line, with the player in front of the line with a ball and all the other players lined up closely one behind the other with their legs open, to allow the ball to be rolled through to the player at the back of the line who crouches down ready to receive the ball. Coach positions themselves just behind the backboard and blows the whistle or says go and the game begins.

Diagram 9b) Once the ball rolls through, the player at the back of the line picks it up and drives to the basket looking to score quickly, then heads back to the front of their teams' line and proceeds to roll the ball through the rest of their teammates legs who've all moved back one place. I usually limit the scoring shot attempts to three to score a basket and help the younger kids by tipping the ball back to them if they miss their shot. Once they get back to the line, they roll the ball through and the drill continues down to the last player who once they've completed their last shot, hustles back to the team and everyone sits on the floor indicating they have finished. If you have too many players just have the last player of one team go through twice and if the teams are a little uneven, you can switch players around or have one team move up close to the free throw line while the other team moves back beyond the centre line if this makes it more competitive.

9a) Set-Up   9b) Rotations

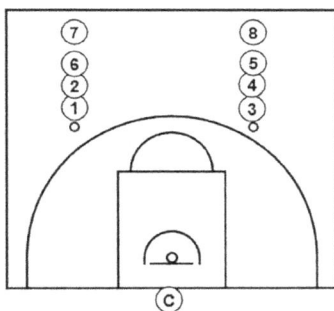 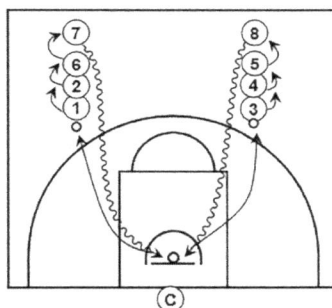

Final Thoughts

There are many games a coach can run at training to bring a much-needed element of fun and the ones listed here are the popular ones we use regularly that complement the game of basketball. Competitive games are challenging and keep players interested whilst also developing footwork, concentration and ball skills.

STRETCHING CHART

Stretching Chart provided by www.stretching.name

Stretching.name

Recommended stretches - Basketball

Stretching routine (exercises guide) recommended for basketball

CHAPTER 6
Team Plays and Structure

CHAPTER 6
TEAM PLAYS AND STRUCTURE

OFFENCE OUTLINE AND CHECKLIST

A simple system of structured plays will help your team become a working unit in a short period of time. These were developed overtime out of necessity to help young players have not only some success with the game, but responsibility and roles that they need to possess to play with other players in the team. What structure does is give players some options rather than having to guess what could happen, but still allowing freedom to think and make decisions within the simple play set. When players have some guidelines in which to work, they actually play far better than they would by just letting them find their way in their own time. Not having to guess too much, and understanding where their teammates will be, will help your young players work better with each other and have confidence that they will provide them a passing, or shot option.

Checklist for Team Plays
- **Split**
- **Out of Bounds – Snakes**
- **Side Ball – Line**

Advanced Plays
- **Out of Bounds – Line**
- **Simple Motion Offence**

THE SPLIT

I truly love the **SPLIT** it has formed the basis of all the **KEY WORDS** I use when teaching beginner players how to play basketball. Now I always used a few **KEY WORDS** as most coaches do but it wasn't until I put them into a system that the rapid improvement of my teams really started to gain ground. The **SPLIT** it is only a one syllable word but when used effectively it will transform your team quite quickly in a short period of time. Teaching players to give each other space in which to work and create good basketball plays will be a process as everything is in basketball. Most coaches will scream "spread out guys" and may use this just a few times at training and then a few more times in the game. I found spread out didn't work so well with really young kids – as many teachers get kids to spread out in lines at school but this is only at arm's length. I use the **SPLIT** all the time at training with beginner players and so do all the coaches at our club and now many coaches of other teams and clubs are starting to pick up on this and also use it. I use it every time our team gets the ball in the game **SPLIT** is the call from the bench and eventually the young players get the idea of creating distance between themselves and the ball. Teaching the **SPLIT** will take a few weeks and you must make this a habit with all your coaching. Whilst teaching the players you constantly stress the main points of emphasis along with continual use of the **KEY WORD SPLIT.**

Part One – Concept of Space (Individual)
Diagram 1a) With the **SPLIT** I stand in front of the team usually in the centre circle with a ball and explain exactly what I want when I yell out **SPLIT**.
Diagram 1b) I ask every player to get away from me and be no closer than 6+ metres but not so far that a six to ten-year-old player wouldn't be able to pass if they are too far away, and get there as quickly as they can to **HUSTLE**.

1a) Set-Up   **1b) SPLIT**

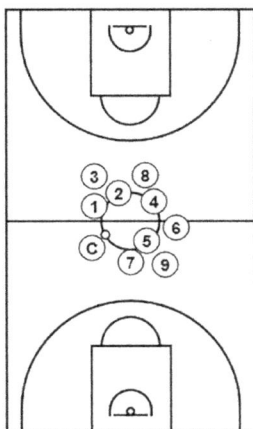 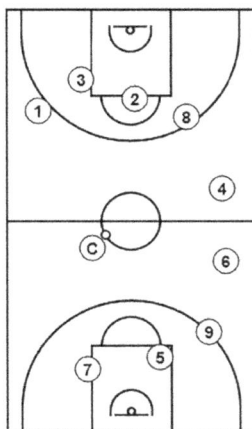

Points of Emphasis on the SPLIT

- Stress that players need to be ready to **SPLIT** as soon as we have the ball

- **HUSTLE** as quickly as possible away from the ball and other teammates

- **ZIGZAG** after eye contact with the passer and lead with a target hand

Diagram 1c) After the players have spread out, I have them **ZIGZAG** back to me not getting any closer than three to four metres with a target hand up and ready for the ball. I expand on this after I correct the first run through, making sure that the players who get too close to me are aware that this will not get them the ball as all they are doing is putting me, their teammate under pressure with their defender being able to pressure me as well. The next thing I explain is that since I have the ball there's no point leading if I am not looking at you. Even if you make a really good lead on a basketball court you will not receive the ball if the player with it is too busy protecting the ball or looking to the other side of the floor. After everyone agrees that this is the correct and a smarter way to play, I then have everyone **SPLIT** away and only **ZIGZAG** when I am looking in their direction. Again, correct the players if they get too close or if they cut too early or it was slow or sloppy. I may repeat this, 10 to 15 times and each time I yell **SPLIT** as they stream away from me and they get into a pattern of **SPLIT** away from the ball, and then **SLOW ZIG** – **FAST ZAG** back to me showing me exactly where they want the ball with a target hand.

1c) SLOW ZAG FAST ZAG - Repeat   1d) Eye Contact - ZIGZAG

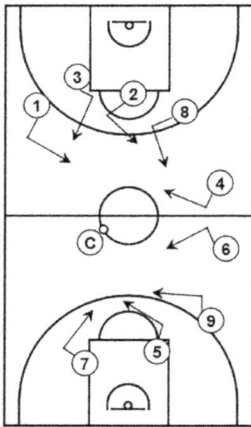

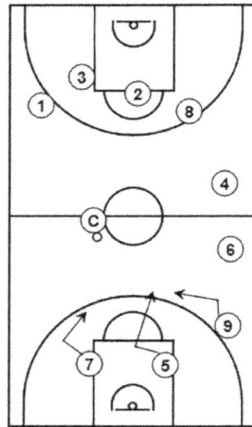

1e) Eye Contact - ZIGZAG   **1f) Eye Contact - ZIGZAG**

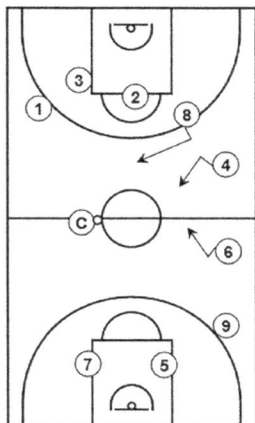

Coach faces players in **Diagram 1d), 1e) and 1f)** and they **ZIGZAG** on eye contact and they must wait until you are looking at them and it's better to be late than early on the **ZIGZAG** lead. This is such an important concept for beginner players to learn that of creating space, movement and of timing leads when a teammate is looking at them and can pass them the ball.

Part Two – Two Player SPLIT
After this I divide the players into pairs with a ball and again practice the split by having the player with the ball yell out **SPLIT** to their teammate. The teammate hustles away then **ZIGZAGS** back with a target hand to make a successful play. If you have a pair of players doing a really good job, blow the whistle stop the squad and ask them to demonstrate the skill to their teammates. Sometimes they may make a mess of it but ask them to do exactly what they showed you the first time and when this happens praise them GREAT JOB and ask the rest of the team to copy what they did. It will take a little time for all the players to get the skill done at a reasonable level and remember coach don't wait for perfection give them the idea and come back to it next training session.

2a) Set-Up Two Players One ball

2b) SPLIT – ZIGZAG

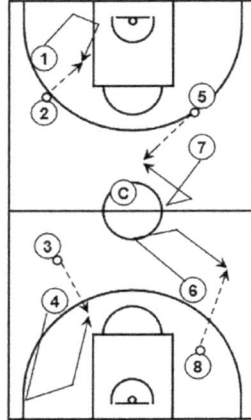

2c) SPLIT – ZIGZAG

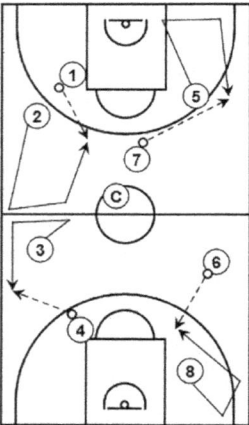

2d) Add Defence

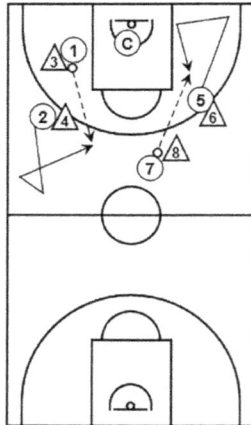

Part Three – Three-player Quarter-court SPLIT

The next drill we progress to is the three-player quarter-court **SPLIT** and it is here I will use three players and usually we run the drill on a quarter of the court. One player has the ball they call **SPLIT** or you can call this out coach or an assistant coach, team manager or helpful parent, the other two players break away from the ball and from each other. Have a huge emphasis coach on plenty of space between the two players away from the ball and then making good **ZIGZAG** cuts with target hands when the player with the ball is looking at them. Coach, please keep your eyes on all the teams performing and give plenty of feedback, correction and encouragement, never fall into the trap of 'they're doing okay I will just watch'. If they're doing well give them a pat on the back or make them demonstrate again for the rest of the group who may be struggling a little with the concept of creating space. This is such an important concept and I often tell players that offence is all about creating space to play and defence is really about reducing the space the team is allowed to play in. You will find by adding the other players that there could be one player tending to stand still or too close to their teammates. Stay the course coach as it may take many sessions before it transfers into the game but it is all a process and build up. Have faith in the process and keep teaching the lesson of space via the **SPLIT** it will really help the kids enjoy the game.

Diagram 3a) Set-up is easy, have the players run the drill in the quarter-court have the player with the ball call out **SPLIT** along with the coach at times if the player forgets or is quiet. You can use a half or full court depending on your numbers and you can also have extra players ready to sub in to get a player out for instruction if they do not quite understand what you need. You can also have everyone watch three players who are doing an excellent job as an example of what we want.

Diagram 3b) Adding defence will confuse players who have become used to easy passing options and suddenly have to negotiate more bodies in the way. Start with hands on shorts defence which allows some successful passes, then add full defence.

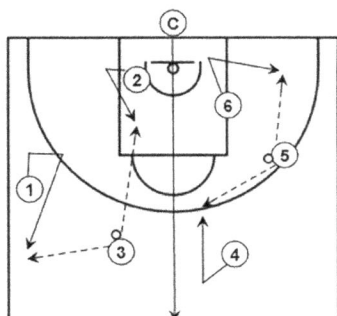

3a) Set-Up   3b) Add Defence

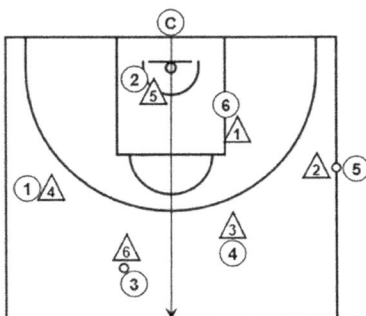

Part Four – Five-player Half-court SPLIT (Keepings Off)
The next step is the five-player **SPLIT** on a half-court with no shots so the ring is not a factor here only the space available on the court. All the players without the ball get away from the player with it and from each other, with quick hustling feet and you the coach keep using the **KEY WORD SPLIT** throughout the entire drill. As you can see, we are really getting players used to the **SPLIT** and conditioning them to react accordingly every time they hear it. Now the five-player **SPLIT** in the half-court is a little different in that we don't want four players leading to the ball at the same time which will create some indecision for the passer or they will just pass to a good friend and ignore other teammates. It is here I get only two players to lead, and then **SPLIT** back out while the other two players lead. With only two leads at a time the decision for the young player with the ball will be simpler and hopefully this will cut down on turn overs.

Diagram 4a) I always start beginner players in a five on zero situation where they can see passing options and break down their leading skills. Now in this diagram I show all four passing options from out of bounds and in court. The reality is you only want one or two players making the initial lead when they get eye contact with the passer, then a secondary lead. Now the reality is it may take several weeks to achieve this and yes there will be crowding of the ball especially when we add defence to the drill. You can run this five on zero drill on a quarter or half-court and it really is an opportunity to drive home the **SPLIT**, spacing and **ZIGZAG** cuts.

4a) Starting Points   4b) Adding Defence – Modified Rules

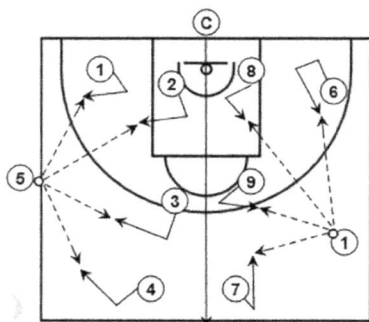

Diagram 4b) Okay coach it is time to add the defence to the drills, and you may have already done this when they are passing in pairs, then in three's and now finally fives. Whenever I add defensive players to a drill, I always start with them keeping their hands on their shorts so it simulates for the players on offence, bodies around them but they can't use their hands to steal the ball. It is important for the defensive players to stay with the matchup they have to guard and it will give them some valuable practice in defence as well as the concept of staying with the same player. Some players will freeze when defence arrives in the drill but you can gently remind them that they must keep their hands on their shorts and cannot touch or steal the ball. Now that the offensive players have an opponent, the emphasis here is to make sure they are leading away from their player and getting open for the ball when their teammate is actually looking at them. It is here you really understand the value of training where you can stop the play and point out corrections and responsibilities, which is impossible to do while in a real game where play is continuous and you have only limited times to give meaningful instruction. It is here I introduce a few rules.

Keepings Off Rules

1. You must pass to a leading player not someone standing still. (Penalty is three to five push-ups for the entire team)

2. You must SPLIT and spread out from the ball. (Penalty for crowding the ball three to five push-ups for entire team)

3. After eight to ten passes the teams change from offence to defence.

Once you have the teams used to defensive bodies being near them and they are running a reasonable **SPLIT** and then a good **ZIGZAG**, you then allow the defensive players to use their hands under the same rules as above with the exception of rule three if the offensive team gets to ten made passes the defensive team does the push-ups, just to create a little motivation for them to stay with their players.

Keepings Off Modified Rules and Additions

• You cannot pass back to the player who passes you the ball, this forces the passer to clear away and create more space for their teammates to lead.

• Add one or two bounces to give the player with the ball more time to find a teammate.

149

- Contact then lead – you cannot pass to a player unless they have made contact with the defence.

- Pass fake then make the pass.

Diagram 4c) & 4d) I now set the team up to attack the basket, now before they can shoot, they must make four to five passes. Coach makes the first pass and you can add the dribble after they make the passes. This is both an offensive and defensive drill and coach can use any and all modified rules.

4c) 5 on 5 Score after 4-5 Passes   **4d) Coach makes first Pass**

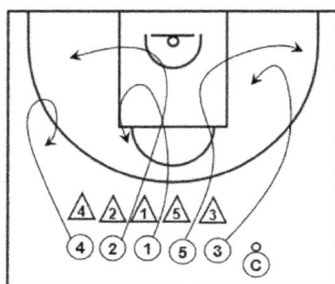

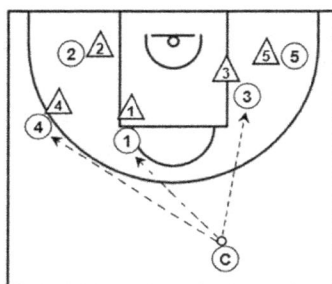

The Split – Full court application
I always impress upon the players that we can be the best shooters in the world, but this would not help the team if we cannot get the ball down the court to actually get some shots up. Using the **SPLIT** full court will be the key component in getting the ball down the floor and hopefully coach, getting up some shots as the real fun part for the players is shooting and scoring baskets. The coach needs to be proactive in the drills and of course use of the word **SPLIT** will be a major factor. Stopping the drills and making corrections helps the players understand that they need to be forward of the ball and in good positions to receive the pass and on a good angle to attack the basket and get the best shots.

Part Five Three-player Full Court SPLIT
Diagram 5a) Have your players form three balanced lines along the baseline with basketballs for every player in the middle line. The coach stands in the

middle of the key and calls out the first three players in line and the player with the ball passes the ball to the coach. Once the three players come out I have them face the basket a few steps back and then ask them to bump each other in the side with their bodies not their elbows to simulate a rebounding contest, as well as get players used to body contact. Now some kids with older siblings will thrive in this environment and will have no problem with the bump and push, others will need your help via such drills to get them used to the eventual contact they will face when ten players are running around in a game, bumping into the opposition players and teammates. Once players have bumped for a few seconds, the coach throws or shoots the ball at the basket trying to miss, calling out the **KEY WORD "BOARDS"** and then the players' battle for the ball to secure the rebound.

Diagram 5b) As soon as one of the players grabs the rebound their 2 teammates must now create out let passes by moving out towards the sidelines. Of course, the coach yells **SPLIT** but it is important players break out to the sides and not down the middle as this will be where the majority of defensive players will be. Once the players are out and in position the rebounder passes out to the out let and then heads off down the floor but along the opposite side.

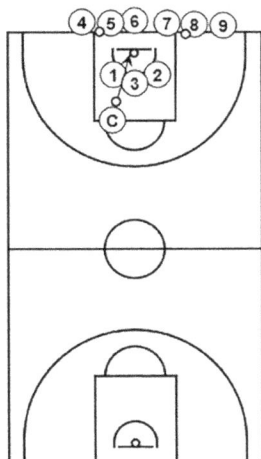

5a) Set-Up   5b) BOARDS SPLIT Outlet PASS

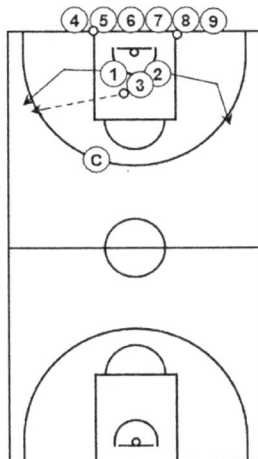

Diagram 5c) The player who receives the ball now has two choices make a further pass down the floor or start a hard drive down the side line drawing the defence off the centre of the court towards them, which will happen as players are always attracted to the ball. The third player who was on the other side will now cut forward to the middle of the court creating a passing option and with the ball on the opposite side-line there shouldn't be too many defensive players around the middle of the floor.

Diagram 5d) Encourage the next pass to the middle of the floor and then that player drives hard towards the free throw line down the split line while their two teammates run the right and left lanes and get ahead of the ball to receive a pass closer to the basket to get a good shot. It will take a few weeks to have the young players working together, keeping good spacing and having a sense of urgency to race the ball down the floor.

5c) DRIVE PASS Run Forward   5d) DRIVE – PASS – PASS – SHOOT

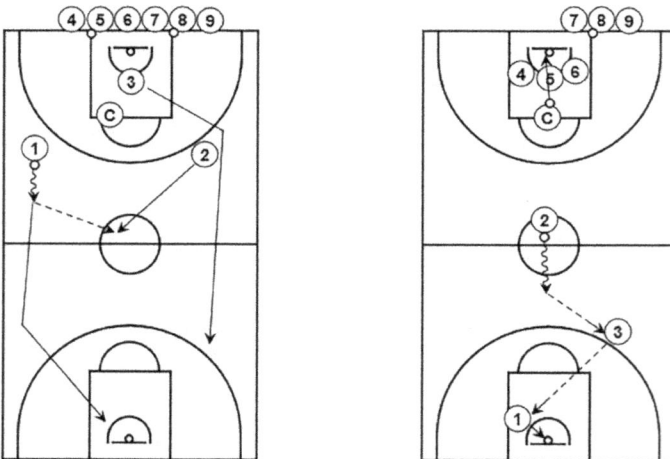

To help train and build this sense of urgency in your players have a time limit that starts once the player makes the first out let pass. Now I will usually make this seven to eight seconds initially with beginners to give them time to get some shots up at the other end of the floor, as they get better with their understanding I will reduce the time and demand they make a basket otherwise a small push-up penalty will result, which is yet another way to give players some extra strength work spread out over the session.

Points of Emphasis for the Three-player SPLIT

- Encourage players to make contact (**BUMP**)
- 2 hands on the rebound (**BOARDS**)
- **SPLIT** to sidelines both sides be ready for the ball
- **DRIVE** hard using outside hand with heads up always ready to pass
- Players must keep running forward and stay in the **SPLIT**
- Shoot good shots

Diagram 5e) As soon as the first team are over the halfway line the next team should be in and ready to go already creating contact with the bump action. After the first team completes the play, they must move off the court to the side-line and stay outside the line on their way back to the starting baseline to resume their rotation. This is an important point because players can get seriously hurt running into each other head on, so it's always safety-first coach and players who get forgetful sometimes need a few push-ups to remind them of the dangers and injury they can cause their teammates. It helps in drills like this that a coach has an assistant coach, team manager or a helpful parent to help the players stay safe and keep the drill moving.

Diagram 5f) Make sure that you practice going both sides of the floor as 90% of players are right-handed so you may find the ball only coming down the right side of the floor on most plays. Really important for the player who receives the pass on the left side and starts driving the ball to use their left hand. As you progress further into the season give the teams a countdown to score and watch the players move the ball down the court faster.

5e) Next Rotation – Side-line Back 5f) Use both sides of the Court

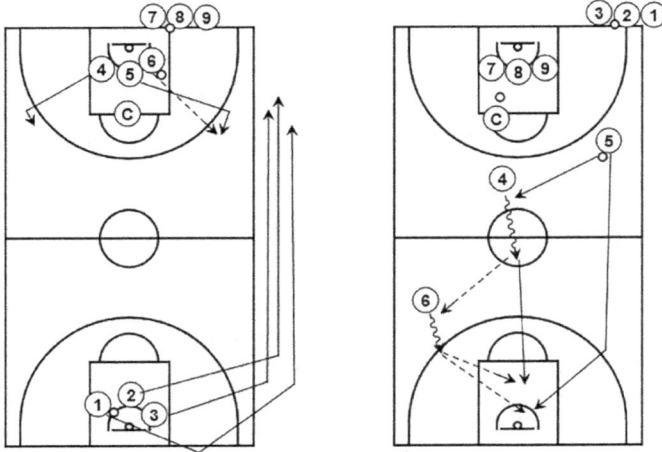

Learning to play full court is the essence of the game as I constantly make young players aware of the fact that all the shooting practice in the world will not help you if you can't get the ball down the floor to actually shoot. This drill is a great start to teach players to work together to bring the ball up the floor and attack the basket. You can throw in one or two defenders once players are comfortable with the drill, the spacing and their skills are improving. The next step is to build up to five players.

Part Six - The Five-player SPLIT
Diagram 6a) 5 lines along the baseline with the basketballs in the middle and the coach takes up the same position as in the three-player **SPLIT**. The five players get close together and again encourage them to bump each other and battle for the rebound.

Diagram 6b) This time as in the three player **SPLIT** once the rebound is secured, two players break out left and right to the out let areas and the other two break out to the side-lines towards the centre line. We now have all players without the ball off the middle of the court creating space for both them and their teammates to lead and cut. Younger players will want to remain down the middle but persist coach, as the rewards will be great as it has been for games I have coached at this level and for my club and its coaches and teams.

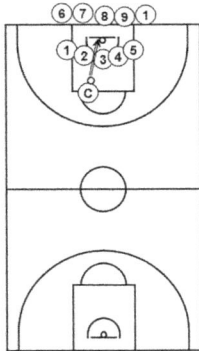

6a) Set-Up   6b) Bump BOARDS SPLIT 6c) Pass DRIVE Pass

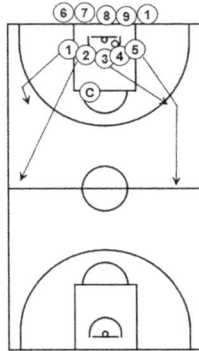

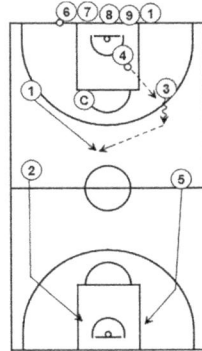

Diagram 6c) Once the outlet player receives the pass, they can again drive the ball forward and they now have the option of passing to the player coming to the middle from the opposite side, but they can also throw a forward pass to teammates who will be heading towards the basket.

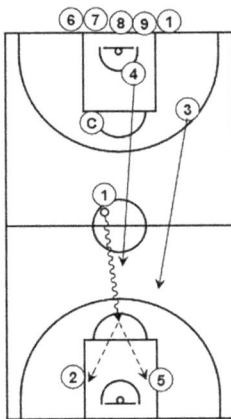

Diagram 6d) The forward pass to the player cutting from the opposite side is always preferable to having a young player receive the ball while running backwards which is difficult and will more than likely result in a travel. With a player receiving the ball in a sideways position they will be able to flow smoothly onto a quick drive down the middle and with their heads up and can make the pass forward if their teammates are open. Once players are getting the concepts and moving the ball well down the floor, impose a time limit to score after the first pass is made. The coach will still be calling **SPLIT** on the rebound and possibly a few extra times if players are too close to each other while pushing the ball down the floor driving rather than dribbling, making quicker passes, **BOARDS** on a missed shot and keep shooting on rebounds. Eventually you want players to be thinking score more so than just happy to shoot, finding good angles and using the back board on the close shots.

Diagram 6e) An important point here is that not all players end up under the basket and in this play four or three should hang back and be the **SAFETY**

player just in case the other team gets the rebound, or we turn it over and need a player to stop an easy run back the other way.

Diagram 6f) All the same points of emphasis made in the three player **SPLIT** applies here and the same **SAFETY** priorities for when the play is over, the players run back outside the court. The coach should wait until the majority of players are off the court before the next team starts.

6e) Floor Balance   6f) Next Rotation

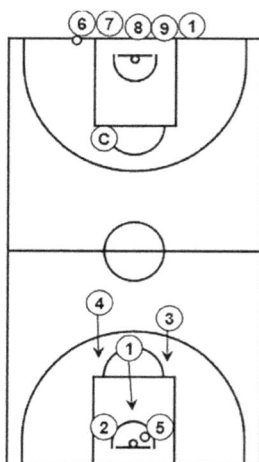

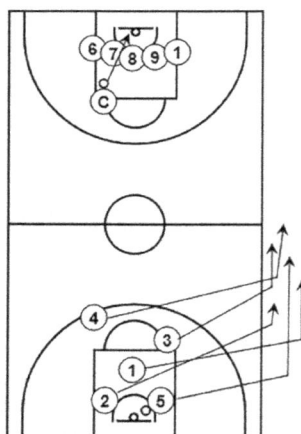

Along with creating a time limit you may also introduce defensive players which will force the offensive players to make decisions on whether to drive, make the pass or shoot when they are in range. Now start with only two defenders and allow them to use their hands and see how your young team negotiates the sudden change from no defence. As they get better, increase the defensive numbers and give out small push-up penalties for throwing silly passes or poor shots.

Final Thoughts On The Split

Is the **SPLIT** the perfect way to get young players to spread out and move the ball down the floor? I would answer possibly not coach, but it is far better than you hoping that the team will be able to do this while working together. You can rely on only one or two players to do all the work ignoring their teammates, but this will only work until you meet the team that will place two or even three defenders pressuring the player who will not trust their teammates nor pass them the ball. The **SPLIT** transformed the way I coached beginner players along with the whole **KEY WORDS** system and having them working together on court. In all honesty if I find something better to use, I will have absolutely no hesitation in using it. As I have mentioned before, it came about after being frustrated with several teams I was working with, how slow our progress was and how poor the games were. It is amazing the answers your brain will come up with when you call on it for solutions to many of the challenges you face on and off the basketball court.

SNAKES – Out of Bounds Baseline Play

SNAKES came about from a basketball camp I worked at many years ago for our State Association for talented Under 12's. I had an opportunity to work alongside some very dedicated, talented coaches whose company I always enjoyed and who I always learnt valuable skills and concepts from, to help my own coaching. It was during a competitive game that a coach ran a simple out of bounds play he called **SNAKES,** whereby all four players started at the three point line then he yelled **GO** and they all made V Cuts to the basket, and if the defence were not too smart and stood beside them as many young players tend to do, they would be left open on a simple cut to the basket for an easy catch and shoot. I loved the play the moment I saw it but thought I could modify it a little to create an element of safety in case the ball was fumbled or stolen. In this simple play, I am already assigning players their roles within the play so they are aware of their responsibilities and what they need to do for the team to create an opportunity to score an easy basket. It is here I also explain the most important players within the **SNAKES** and it might surprise a few that it is not the player who scores the basket although, they will be the happiest once they achieve this.

Diagram S1) shows the starting point for the **SNAKES** play. The coach stands by the team's best smaller player passer and acts like a referee ready to hand them the ball.

Player **(2)** – The most important player on the court is the **SAFETY**. If something goes wrong, they are the last line of our defence and must not go inside the free throw line on this particular play. As the three players cut to the basket, they can cut towards the elbow as they may receive the ball if the entire defence collapses into the basket. From here it is a simple free throw if they're open or they can pass the ball to a teammate in a better position.

Player **(1)** – The second most important player, as their decision can make a great, average or poor play as they will make the pass. Make the passer understand that we are looking to get the ball to a teammate in a great shooting position close to the basket.

Diagram S3). If the scoring passes are not available, hang on to the ball and wait for a teammate to then lead into open space. Always insist on making a safe pass as without the ball we can't shoot or score and it is important that the young player is aware of this.

Players **(3)**, **(4)** and **(5)** – Usually the biggest or best shooting players take these three positions and make a strong **ZIGZAG** cut to the basket in **Diagram S2)** when the coach says go. Always have your best rebounders take one or more of the positions to increase the chance of rebounding on a missed shot attempt. The players cutting to the basket must understand that if they do not get the ball then they must lead away from the basket in a quick attempt to get open for the ball **Diagram S4)** as the passer only has five seconds or in most cases the referees will give them some extra time as they are only beginners. Running a quick split is far better than having all your players standing stationary with their opponents' right beside them looking to steal the ball.

Points of Emphasis for SNAKES
- Set-up quickly and make sure everyone is outside the three-point line
- Encourage the passer to throw strong chest and bounce passes
- Cut hard into shooting positions
- Make sure the safety is in a position to shoot from the elbow
- Everyone waits for the coach to calls out **GO**

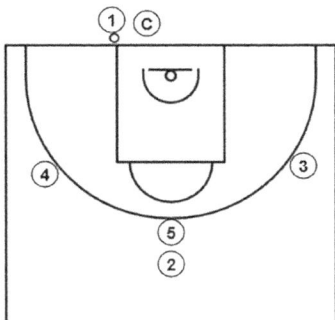

S1) Set-Up   **S2) 3 Cuts to the Basket + a Safety**

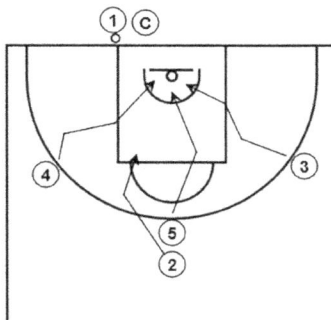

S3) Scoring Options   **S4) Breakdown Option**

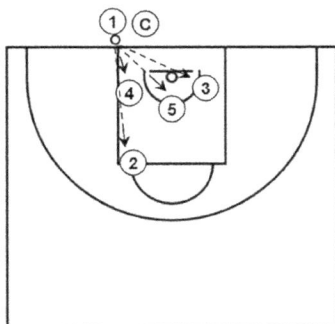

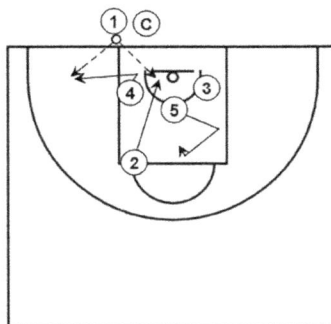

Add defence to the drill once players are comfortable with the play set and have them play hands on shorts in the initial stages of learning the play. Of course, coach you can modify this play to change it up a little as your players get a little more experienced and the opposition gets a little better at defending it. I would start with this simple version of **SNAKES** first and to be honest I haven't made too many variations as it really works well even if defence stands off your players a little, there is always one that will forget to guard their player which allows you to cut around them for a successful play and a possible basket.

I run this play straight into a five-player SPLIT and practice two phases of offence at the same time giving players an opportunity to run both in combination.

LINE – Out of Bounds Side-line Play

LINE – side-line plays have been around as long as basketball and they are great way to introduce your players to some simple structure in which they can work with their teammates and yet give them plenty of freedom to make decisions. This play is simple enough and your only real problem, apart from the forgetful youngster who races off down the court way too early, is having the line stand back far enough to create the initial space in which to lead for the ball.

Diagram L1) A simple enough starting point for the players as everyone knows what a line is, so getting in the setup shouldn't be too hard. I have the first player in line either line up with the keys or the three circles clearly marked out on the court. The coach stands beside the passer with the ball to simulate what a referee will do before handing the ball to them. Again, it must be stressed to the players their roles in the play and of the importance of each player within the structure.

Diagram L2) Player **(2)** – The most important player in the LINE, they will initially head one or two steps towards our basket then cut back behind players **(1)**, **(5)** and **(3)** and act as both a safety and a secondary receiver. Player **(4)** – The passer must make good decisions on this play so place not only a good passer here but a strong passer as they are looking to throw the ball long to **(1)**, **(5)** and **(3)** who will be taking off down the floor towards your basket in an attempt to jump the defence and gain an advantage. Player **(1)**, **(5)** and **(3)** – All three players will start the play by taking two to three steps back towards their opponent's basket and then take off as fast as they can towards our basket looking to gain an advantage and create an easy scoring opportunity. Place your best driver and most competent ball handler in front, but give all players a chance to play this spot just in case that player is on the bench or not playing, which will happen over the course of a season. I have all players rotate through all positions just to give them a better understanding of the play, however in a game I want a strong passer to throw the ball in as the play really depends on this when the defence is caught chasing us from behind.

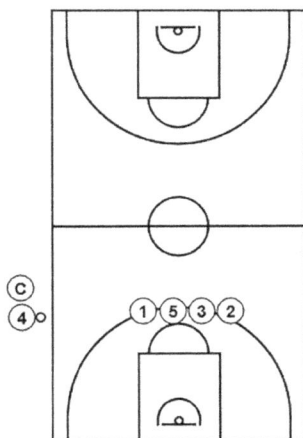

L1) Set-Up   **L2) First Stage**

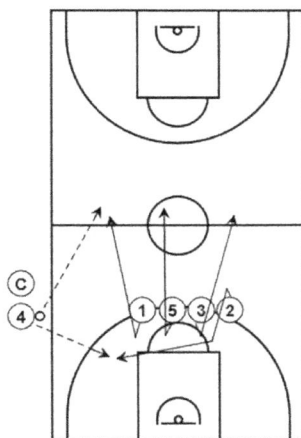

Diagram L3), L4) The opposition will eventually place a **SAFETY** player back and this is okay as we just shorten the pass to **(1)** and still attack with all three players. Once the ball has been thrown forward players **(4)** and **(2)** trail down behind **(1)**, **(5)** and **(3)** and act as both safeties and receivers if the play is broken up by the defence.

L3) Passing Forward Options   **L4) Passing Backwards Options**

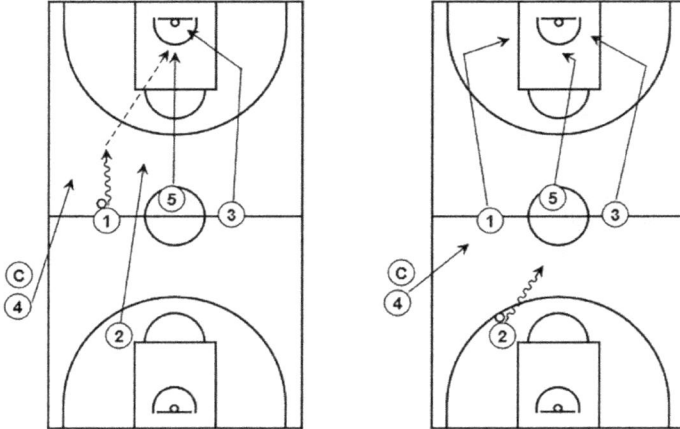

Points of Emphasis

- Make sure coach that you practice variations including

- Passing the ball long and forward for players to run onto

- Passing the ball forward and short, just in case there is a safety player from the opposition waiting for you

- Passing the ball backwards to the safety who brings it down the court

- Passing it to the safety **(Player 2)** who then passes back to the passer **(Player 4)** heading forward and is inside the court

- No passes available and players must now **ZIGZAG** back to the ball to get open

Now the variations will all need to be practiced at a later stage, all you need do in the beginning is pass forward and make sure that they start in the line and then **GO** on your command, and have a safety player which is a must. The line naturally runs into the split and a little practice at each session will create a great weapon for the team, but as with everything don't labour to long looking for perfection.

The LINE can really take advantage of defenders who lose their player or stands to close to the offence and get caught out when they break down the floor. Repetition here will be important at both training and games to really make the play work and remember coach to have your tactic board with you at training and games. I always find with younger players that they will crowd the side-lines even if they are in a **LINE. BACK UP** may be a **KEY WORD** you will need to use until the starting point is further away from the passer, creating the space for the play to function better.

Diagram L5), L6) When attacking the basket, its important players stay in the **SPLIT,** look towards the basket with the ball in their hands, find the open player with a safe pass and drive the ball hard.

L5) Pass/Drive/Pass/Shot   **L6) Good Floor Balance**
Safety/Boards

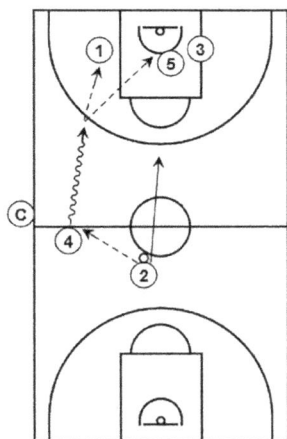

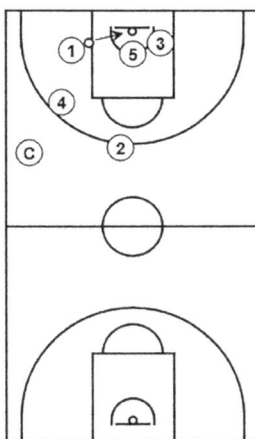

Points of Emphasis on the LINE

- Set-up quickly
- Wait for the **GO** call
- Stay in the **SPLIT**
- Always look for the next pass
- Make sure we have a safety player
- Move the ball as fast as possible and shoot good shots

Final Thoughts
Introduce the simple plays and structure early in a training session, as tired bodies will learn very little, so introducing new things at the end of a training session will not be very productive with little retained by young athletes. I would teach **SNAKES,** and **LINE** in the first half of the session and make sure you cover it at every training session after the first introduction until it is running reasonably well in games. I have a magnetic coaching board and I sit the players in a small tight circle on the floor where we run the play with the magnetic figures and I give some of our players a chance to explain the plays to their teammates. We then head back onto the floor and run the plays, rotating all the players through the various spots to help them understand what they and their teammates have to do. Working within the age group will never be a complete science as so many factors will come into play but usually around the six to eight weeks mark the team starts to play a reasonable brand of basketball in regards to working together in this simple system of plays.

ADVANCED PLAYS

Advanced Plays for Older Beginners
If you're working with older beginner players then these introductory advanced plays will be a great introduction to simple play sets and offensive structure. This is just like learning a language that will forever expand as players and coaches move through the different levels and gain valuable experience. It is also here that the coach introduces screening, which involves an offensive player standing still and creating a blocking action so that their teammates can run their defensive player into this to create a scoring option, or frees a player up for an easy pass.

SETTING SCREENS

As we move to more advanced play, both coaches and players will need to understand how to set and use screens. I find players have little problem setting screens - it is the habit of using them that will need attention to detail and a little time. The stance for setting screens differs between boys and girls and it is important that both protect their soft tissue areas.

Boys – must protect their lower groin area as players setting screens may come into contact with a swinging arm, leg or hip as the defensive player gets caught on the screen. The player pictured on the left is in the correct stance, which is for the player to grab their right wrist with their left hand, and set the feet shoulder width apart and brace down with knees slightly bent. The player on the right with the crossed hands is in the incorrect position. The cross hands position can leave a player with pinned arms after contact and falling backwards without the ability to throw the arms out to break the fall could cause serious injury.

Girls - should protect their chest area as heavy contact can result from arms shoulders and body checks as a result of defensive players trying to stay with the player they are guarding. The player pictured on the right is in the correct stance with arms bent and hands are made into fists pointing in to the inside of the shoulders, which brings tension to the arms and the player braces down with feet shoulder width apart and knees slightly bent in readiness for possible contact. The player on the left with crossed arms is in a poor position to take contact and unlike the player on the right, will not be able to break their fall by freeing their arms out to break their fall. This is not a small point and players must understand that setting screens the wrong way can lead to falling back and hitting their head on the floor.

As with all basic basketball skills, setting the screen the right way must become a habit and players must always protect their bodies as the defensive player in their effort to stay with their assigned player, who will sometimes cause very heavy contact, and some of the time be unaware a screen is even being set on them. The next phase after the correct stance is formed is screening angles for teammates to use the screen.

USING THE SCREEN

Once players have the basics of correct stance for setting screens the next phase is teaching screening angles to best help their teammates get open, along with showing players the best technique to help them use the screen to get open. The pictures below show player number **25** using the **SLOW ZIG - FAST ZAG** cut from left to right, rubbing shoulders with the player setting the screen to get into open space. Players must learn that basketball is a contact game and when setting and using screens plenty of contact will occur. The SLOW ZIG is all about making contact with the defensive player and then freezing them by stopping suddenly then exploding on the FAST ZAG to move away from them and rubbing shoulders with the screener, not allowing any space to get through and forcing them to either go under or over the screener, or even being jammed up on the screen. Either way the offensive player should have a window in which to get free and create some space for a pass and a possible scoring option. An important point on setting screens is the screener cannot move until their teammate has rubbed shoulders and moved away from them, as this is an offensive foul if you're moving while setting the screen. The player using the screen must also wait until the screener is stationary and not be impatient and move too early. A good way to make sure you don't get offensive fouls on screens being set is for the player setting the screen to call out to a teammate "GO" when they are still and in good position. Once players have the good screen set and use the footwork to get open, we then can add defence. I always have the defence start with their hands on their shorts to stop passes being deflected or stolen and giving the offence a better chance to execute the skills without the pressure of losing the ball.

Set-Up   SLOW ZIG   FAST ZAG   Shoulder Rub Add Defence

Setting and using screens will eventually become a strong foundation for effectively freeing players up and it also promotes great teamwork. You can also have players who are a little behind the skill set of their teammates help free up your most effective offensive players and make a huge contribution to a team's success.

Points of Emphasis for Screening

- Use the correct stance and no crossed arms

- Set the screen on the angle that makes you the widest target for your teammate

- Hold the screen until your teammate has passed you without moving

- Set the cut up by moving into the defender with a **SLOW ZIG**

- Cut hard with a **FAST ZAG** and rub shoulders with the screener

LINE - BASELINE OUT OF BOUNDS PLAY

With older beginners **SNAKES** is a great play to start with but I like to introduce this play as it has many elements and attacking offensive options. It is also a great play to lead into running five player half court offensive sets, as each player here can create a shot option so long as they not only run the play but also penalise the defence when they try to cheat and adjust to stop that particular scoring option.

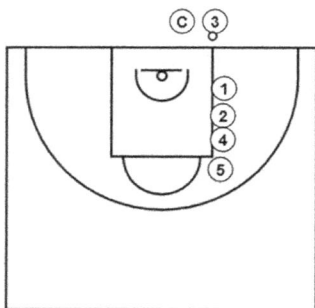

Diagram L1) The set-up for the play is really easy and the players should have no problems getting in a line and the really great aspect is that the line runs along the side of the key using the markings that separates the players during free throws. **(1)** should be the smallest player of the five and starts at the block which is the second marker along the edge of the key from the baseline. **(2)** is the best mid-range shooter and lines up on the next marker. **(4)** is usually the second tallest player and a strong rebounder and good slash cutter. **(5)** the biggest player starts at the back of the line at the elbow which is the corner of the free throw line. **(3)** the passer should stand back from the baseline at least two steps to allow them a step forward to make a strong pass and be back far enough to not let a defensive player intimidate or place strong pressure on the ball. The play starts with the coach or **(3)** calling out **GO** or a simple ball slap can also key this. **(4)** makes a slash cut to the opposite side of the basket while **(2)** pops out to the short corner within their shooting range.

Diagram L2) Once **(4)** and **(2)** have made their cuts this opens up space for **(1)** to set a back screen for **(5)** who then cuts hard to the basket making sure they **ZIGZAG** forcing their defensive players into the screen. If **(5)** is able to run their defensive player into the screen it sets up the classic mismatch option of a taller player against a smaller player if the defence switch players close to the basket giving the offence a definite advantage in a prime scoring position. **(4)** can also step outside the key and then cut back underneath re-establishing position to take a second bite, especially if the defence played it well on the first cut. Occasionally **(5)** will get jammed up unable to use **(1)** screen so this is a great second option.

Diagram L3) (3) has 4 passing options here for players to get great shots with very strong rebounding options if the shot misses. **(1)** after setting the screen flares or curls to a scoring position but also a defensive covering position to make sure the opposition doesn't get away for an easy fast break score. They are also in a point position to run half-court offence here if the play breaks down. **(3)** should keep the defensive players off balance by pass faking this will also open up great angles for scoring passes especially bounce passes. **(2)** should also be active just in case three to four seconds pass and they need to step in and out to get open for a pass to avoid a five second violation. **(4)** and **(5)** need to brace down and be strong to hold these prime rebounding positions.

Diagram L4) This play can be very effective if run well with strong cuts and good timing and passing and will have the defence making adjustments to stop players scoring easy shots. To counter inside scoring options often the player guarding **(3)** will drop back under the basket with no pressure on the ball. It is here **(3)** can make a quick pass to **(2)** and then cut into the open gap for a short range shot before **(5)** cuts into the basket. **(3)** can also pass out to **(1)** and then cut out behind **(2)** for a screened protected shot.

Final Thoughts

I always introduce this play first before I advance to half-court offence as this simple play helps players establish roles and responsibilities while playing the various positions on the line. It also introduces screening, posting up close to the basket, cutting for a purpose to attack the basket and make position to score, working with teammates by timing cuts and sequencing the play to create the best options to score. I spent many hours looking at various baseline out of bounds plays before structuring this and it has been responsible for creating scoring shots against many opponents. I would encourage you to experiment with change up, cuts and mixing the players in the line to take advantage of various strengths and opponent's weaknesses.

SIMPLE MOTION OFFENCE

When I started playing basketball, I was in my first year of High School and had one of the best coaches in my home State and in my humble opinion the country. Now you may be a coach of older beginner players and once they get past the basic structures and are getting a good understanding of rules and are moving forward with their basic skills then it is a good time to introduce a basic man to man offence. Offence can take many forms, from simple to the complex and then there are special plays for every conceivable situation and time that occurs during the game. Now for your just-past-beginner players an offence that can be executed on some simple key words fits really well with the rest of the concepts in this book. This is a continuity offence which means it can repeat itself over and over until a good scoring option presents itself.

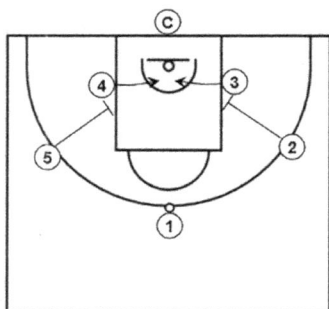

Diagram M1) The setup requires player **(1)** at the top (point position) with the ball and **(2)** and **(5)** starting wide on the wings level with the free throw line and **(4)** and **(3)** on the block on the edge of the key opposite each other keeping good spacing and floor balance. The coach calls out the first of the **KEY WORDS PINCH** in which **(4)** and **(3)** take a post-up widespread position together close to the basket trying to front the defensive players to open up a pass and scoring opportunity especially if both defenders are caught playing from behind. The second set of KEY WORDS which gets the players in motion is **DOWN SCREEN** where both **(5)** and **(2)** set a screen positioning themselves in a static position on the edge of the key near the block.

Diagram M2) From the **PINCH** position **(4)** and **(3)** lead out using the screens set by **(5)** and **(2)** leading out to the wings underneath the two screening players. **(1)** Can also drive the ball around their opponent and look for the short range shot if they feel they can easily beat their defensive opponent but in the early stages of teaching the offence it is important that we involve all the players so everyone can both move and learn. It is important that **(1)** keeps dribbling the ball (also known as keeping the ball alive) until a passing option presents itself. Here the pass is made to the right wing to **(3)** and for some strategic value I place the two tallest players on the left-hand side of the floor and a smaller player **(2)** sets the initial screen, which sets up the play beautifully for mismatches in height close to the basket and around the free throw area for a mid and short-range shot.

Diagram M3) On receiving the ball **(3)** tucks the ball onto the front of the hip and then turns and faces the basket in a triple threat stance. Once **(3)** is facing the basket they should use pass fakes and dribble fakes to keep the defensive opponent off balance to open up an easy pass to teammates. While **(3)** is occupying their opponent **(2)** and **(1)** set **AWAY SCREEN**'s on the defensive opponents guarding **(5)** and **(4)**. These away screens also called cross screens are designed to either create two scoring options or mismatch situations mainly a taller player on a smaller player. The two players **(2)** and **(3)** need to set the screens on good angles so that **(5)** and **(4)** can V cut their defensive player into the screen rubbing shoulders with screener not allowing the defensive player any space to slide through with the cutter. The cuts here follow the same technique of the **SLOW ZIG-FAST ZAG** except this time the slow part directs the defensive player in a slowly in one direction until it is followed by a strong cut to free the player up for an open shot. The cutters must also make sure that **(3)** is actually looking at them when they cut so the pass can be completed or at the very least attempted. As I tell all players I work with you can make the best and most open cut in the world and yet the passer is being pressured and their focus is on protecting the ball than looking to make a scoring pass. This is why the passer (3) must keep the defensive player off balance to open up an easy pass.

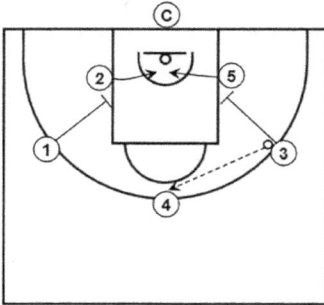

Diagram M4) As I stated in the first paragraph this offence is a continuity offence which means it runs continuously back into itself so the players can keep running it multiple times over. In the previous diagram player (4) attacked the free throw line on the cut but neither (4) or (5) was able to receive a pass to score so (4) pops out to the top to receive a pass from (3) and (1), (2) and (5) make small adjustments in position to reset the offence and start over with the call of **PINCH, DOWN SCREEN, LEAD OUT, SCREEN AWAY. SLOW ZIG FAST ZAG** sums up the offence with **KEY WORDS.** As you can see in this diagram (4) now controls the offence from the top and must now make decisions on which player to pass to for the best strategic advantage for the team. This is a great part of basketball in that you can have a structured offence to run and yet the players must still make independent decisions that show where their thinking is in relation to the game. I like to get as many possible mismatches as I can close to the basket so I teach the players to base the wing pass on what will happen after the **DOWN SCREEN.**

Players Love to dribble the ball and these two diagrams show both the point player (1) and the wing players have the freedom to do this providing they are not running into a mass of defenders or their teammates.

Diagram M5) Here we have the point player driving hard down the middle of the floor now they have several options in which they decide.

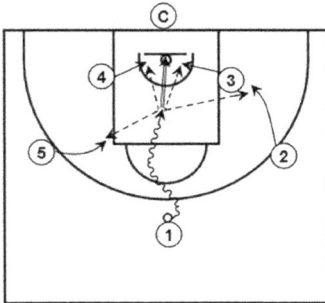

1) Shoot the ball at the free throw line or just inside the key before they run into other defenders.
2) Draw the defenders to them who are helping their teammate who has been beaten but they themselves are now leaving their players which provides multiple passing options. Here players **(2)**, **(3)**, **(4)** and **(5)** are moving into various positions to get free for shots, but more importantly giving the point player **(1)** options to make a great play. Coaches you may want to slow this down and explore these and many other options based on which defender helps out at the time.

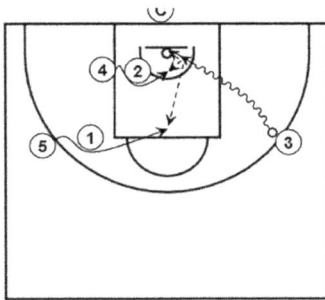

Diagram M6) In this passage the wing player **(3)** drives to the basket and we can explore all the shot options this presents which can be far more than the point player especially as the help defence will not be in as good a position based on the screening players.

1) Although I have diagrammed a hard drive to the basket here **(3)** can drive either side of the defender pulling up for shot range shots having the whole side of the floor present multiple opportunities.
2) Similar to the point driving the ball, as defenders come off their assigned players to try and stop **(3)** their teammates **(2)**, **(4)**, **(5)** and **(1)** can reposition themselves to take advantage of an open shot. Coaches break this down and show the players where they can get shots before adding defence.

Adding defence will be the next step and I want to help the players get used to this before we let them play a full scrimmage. We start with quarter-court offence and have the defensive players hold their shorts so they can't steal the ball, this allows the offensive players the freedom to play without losing the ball. It's amazing how quickly players will forget what needs to be done in this offence when they're suddenly confronted by players standing in front or beside them even if they can't use their hands. This also allows players to run the offence through several times getting used to the motion and learning to set and use screens. Once players are feeling comfortable running the offence against the hands on shorts defence we then allow the defence to use their hands but often make the defenders guarding the ball to back up a little to allow the opportunity for the player to make passes to the players coming off the screens before we play full out.

Expect players will make mistakes when trying to run this in games as they will be a little hesitant at times and feel they must pass to a teammate and it may even cost a team a few victories initially, but just like learning a language once this basics structure is learnt so many more options and plays can be added. It is important to be patient here coach and providing players are making progress be it fast or slow in the long run it will only benefit the team and teamwork especially when confronted by teams that play really good man to man defence. As I said it is like learning a new language and kids will amaze you at how they pick things up.

As a follow up to this book, I will be releasing the next phase in a players development bridging the gap between the beginner starting out and the more advanced and elite player and team. This will help prepare them for far more experienced opponents and competition, with the tools for greater skill development and we build on this and many other offences and plays. For now this simple motion play will get the team started on building a more structured offence for the side and yet it does have opportunities for players to make independent decisions based on where teammates are and if they drive the ball at opportune times.

CHAPTER 7
Game Coaching

CHAPTER 7
GAME COACHING

INTRODUCTION AND STARTING POINTS

Okay coach you've had one or several training sessions in preparation for your very first game. Unfortunately, competitive basketball is the opposite of the classroom because you get the test first and the lesson second. In school, you get several lessons and practice tests before you get the real test. In a real game of basketball everything that is happening out there is a test, some players learn these lessons quickly and others may take weeks and even seasons. Uncertainty is the part of basketball you have no control over, and beginners will still be coming to terms with the rules so don't be surprised if there are a few confused players on the floor. The game is so fluid and your players can improve so much in such a short period of time provided you can teach and encourage them.

During the game, it is important to stay focused on your team playing winning basketball, having fun and not so much on winning the game. Even though some of your players will want to win every time they play and you may have a superior team to your opposition that day based purely on athleticism and height and simply over power them, yet play quite poorly. I tell many of the players I coach the scoreboard can tell many lies as you may be playing really great team basketball yet be missing many shots on the day. You may also throw up some terrible shots and get lucky and win almost by default. It is here you will find out just how effective your message at training is in the way the team actually plays, not what the scoreboard is telling someone who may have just walked in to the stadium.

With the **KEY WORDS,** you have worked on at training guiding your team, you will start to see many of these words taking effect as the players react to them during the game. **KEY WORD** coaching will transform your beginner players into a working unit and it is really important that you stay consistent with your message and your training. It is so easy for a coach to say they are playing well now and go away from the process that made the improvement and relax but just like the players you must keep working on your own habits. The attention-span of your players will be limited especially the younger ones,

KEY WORDS will play a big part in keeping them focused. I think by now you understand that coaching a team of young beginner athletes will require that you do far more than just turn up and call substitutions. As discussed in a previous chapter there are several roles as a coach that you are now empowered to act on. Let us look at a checklist of what is required as coach that you will need during game.

COACHES CHECKLIST

- **Pre-game address**
- **Selecting a starting five**
- **Game coaching and developing your team and voice**
- **Time outs**
- **Half time breaks**
- **Post-game address**

PRE-GAME ADDRESS

With younger players, there is no need to have big pre-game speech full of fire and brimstone and a complicated strategic plan. Keep it fun and simple coach! Emphasis should be placed on all the things we are working on at in training, not on the result of this yet-to-be played game. In the first game, you will be explaining which way the team is going in each half and asking players to remember things like not running with the ball without bouncing it, make sure we pass to the boys or girls with the same coloured uniforms and picking up the opposition players when they have the ball.

Here is an example pre-game talk for a team of kids that have never played before and it is addressing boys but both can easily be used for both sexes. I like to ask a few questions of the players and get them thinking about what they need to do. **Really important to have a coaching tactics board so you can utilise visual communication as well as verbal.**

"Hi Team how are we feeling?"
From this simple question, you will see that some of the players are nervous, excited, anxious, worried, scared and some may be very calm having no idea what is going to happen. You the coach may be feeling all these emotions as well.

"Okay Jimmy, Greg, Rod, Charlie and Robby will be starting on the court and John, Michael and Mark will sit with me on the bench. Today we are playing our first game of basketball and we need to remember a few things that we did at training."
It is here that you will get them thinking about simple tasks they need to perform during the game and get their minds focused on tasks they need to do rather than all the emotions they may be feeling.

"Whatever way Jimmy is facing at the jump ball is the way we will go in the first half and the basket we will be shooting at. Now if we are shooting at that basket what do we need to do at the other end?"
Some players here will know the answer and others may be a little confused.

"Yes, that's right Greg we'll be playing defence and trying to stop the other team scoring."
 Simple questions are great at this time to relax players as believe me they will all be a little nervous.

"Are we allowed to run with the ball?"
Usually you will get a big no from most of the players.

 "Yes, that's right Mark we need to bounce or dribble the ball if we want to move somewhere with it."
"And what if I stop dribbling with the ball what can I do then?"
Again, there will be a few players who know and some players that will give you a blank stare or two.

"That's correct John we can pass or shoot at the basket if we are close enough." Now we can build on this a little further.

"What if I am being guarded closely and pressured by an opposition player, what can I do now to protect the ball from them?"
This is important as it will happen throughout the game.

"Yes, Jimmy that's correct we must pivot and keep the ball away from them. Can everyone show me how we pivot please and protect the ball?"
I get all players now to demonstrate pivoting and even have them pair up to simulate the defender's pressure so they understand what is going to happen.

"**Before we dribble the ball, we should look for a pass first and remember keep pivoting and protecting the ball and if you do dribble, let's make sure we have our eyes up so we can see our teammates ahead of us. Who else should we keep our eyes on as well as our teammates?**"
A good question to help the players focus on the fact we are playing another team.

"**Now let's say Jimmy needs to pass the ball, what should the other four players do? Should they stand there and watch Jimmy or ZIGZAG and get open for the ball?**" Most players will tell you they should **ZIGZAG** and this is another great opportunity to have them demonstrate a V cut for you. Pick up a warm up ball have them **SPLIT** away from you and then lead back showing a target hand as they do. Do this several times and hopefully but not always you may see it happen during the game. I am also using two **KEY WORDS** here that I will use during the game **SPLIT** and **ZIGZAG**.

"**Okay team how many players will start on the court for us?**
"**Yes, that is correct five and how many will start on the court for the other team? Correct five so how many players does each of you need to guard when we don't have the ball? Only one that's correct. Now can everyone count to one?**"

I always get agreement when I ask this simple question, can you count to one?

"**Excellent then we can all play defence as that is all I need you to do is guard one player and remember you must be close enough to touch them when they are close to their basket and could get a shot up. If they are close to the basket with the ball, what must we do then?**"
Here is another opportunity to introduce another key word you will use quite a lot when on defence **SMOTHER**.

"**We must SMOTHER the ball when the player is close enough to shoot a basket and can everyone show me a defensive stance please.**"

I have everyone demonstrate their defensive stance and then step up and **SMOTHER** in pairs with 1 player pretending to shoot. Make sure the players are standing straight up with finger slightly curled towards their partners.

"Okay every time we get the ball remember to SPLIT away from it and ZIGZAG back to get open for the pass. Keep your head and eyes up when you do dribble and make sure we are always looking for the forward pass. On defence, we guard only one player, ONE EACH and make sure we get in the stance and are not leaving our player to ball chase. When the player you're guarding is close enough to shoot remember to SMOTHER. Now everyone, get out there and have some fun and remember the simple things I need you to do. If you make a mistake, forget about it, it is not a problem just keep playing and let us all learn how to play together as a team. This is really what we are doing this season is learning how to play winning basketball and not worrying about winning games. Hands in, have fun guys 3, 2, 1 TEAM."

At my club, we are called Central City Breakers, so rather than do 1 2 3 or 3 2 1 Team I call out "Central City" and the players yell "Breakers" and if your team has a two or three-part name you can do a similar chant. In our summer season, we always put hands in on top of mine. In winter however when colds, flu's or gastric viruses are present, everyone puts a fist into the middle of the huddle without actually touching and then chant, to safeguard against spreading anything through the entire team. I also encourage parents to keep infected players away from training and games if this is the case.

This will be enough for your first game and your players will for most parts have no idea what their supposed to be doing in regards to the finer points of playing the game. Remember to reassure them that it's okay to make mistakes as we are all learning the game and everyone and the team will get much better as we learn at training how to play winning basketball.

SELECTING A STARTING FIVE

The choice of a starting five will be far more important to your players than to you. I remember a great high school coach from America, once stating it really doesn't matter who starts, so long as we have a lot of finishers. During the regular season, I have an equal court time policy and will rotate as many players as I can through the stating five.

Now every team has various levels of ability and over the course of a season this can change quite significantly. Players have different motivations in regards to training and also there are always differences in athleticism and size. I try as much as possible to not start the best five players, preferring to have strong players on the bench that can come in and keep momentum or make an impact. I've watched many coaches hurt their teams by having their most inexperienced line up on for extended periods having subbed out several of the strongest players pretty much throwing the game away and driving down the confidence of the group. Always keep a balanced line up on as much as you possibly can and preach playing winning basketball over winning games. As this is a team of beginners rotate the starting five every week again keeping in mind all of the above points. It is certainly okay to have your best team on in the last few minutes in a close game to help you be competitive and possibly win the game, but winning is always secondary to developing kids as players and a team at this level.

Warm Up
Before the game starts you will get a very brief period of time to warm the team up in readiness to play. This will vary from only two to five minutes in most leagues and longer if you're the first game of the day, so it is vital to use this to get as many shots up as you can and do your jogging, stretching, passing, leading and dribbling in a pre-warm up before you get to the court. Make sure your players shoot both layups and some short- range shots and if time permits some free throws and create a small routine they can do at practice. I have covered warm ups in the chapter on training plans, where you can take various drills and add them to create a routine that gets players game ready.

Game Time
Okay the referees have called your team into the opening jump ball; the young players have many mixed emotions right now especially if it's the very first game they have ever played. You may need to go on to the court to quickly arrange them and let them know which way they are going on offence once the ball is tapped. After this the game will get into its ebbs and flows and there will be at times mass confusion as all these little people try and work out what is going on.

Really important here coach is that you're teaching them the difference between offence and defence and yes you will need to be very vocal. Unless some of the kids have played before the mistakes will come thick and fast and there will most likely be a mass of bodies in close range to the ball pretty much for a majority to the game. If your voice isn't projecting to reach the players get some help from a parent, friend, or anyone really that can help ram home the key words to your players. Long winded sentences from the coach from the bench during this time will not get through to the young players out on the court. **KEY WORDS** are the most effective way to reach the players.

KEY WORDS FOR GAMES

Offence

- **SPLIT** – players break away from the ball

- **ZIGZAG** – a simple V cut back to the ball **SLOW ZIG** and a **FAST ZAG** with a target hand creating a passing lane to receive the ball

- **RIP IT** – when the situation of two opposing players getting their hands on the ball at the same time, I call out **RIP IT** which encourages our player to not just be content to get a jump ball but really be aggressive in controlling the ball

- **NEXT PASS** – this lets the player with the ball know they need to be looking for teammates

- **DRIVE** – I prefer players **DRIVE** rather than dribble. Driving the ball gets players moving forward as well as the ball and has real energy to it.

- **GIVE IT** – tells the player with the ball there is a forward pass available and they need to move the ball on

- **HEADS UP** – this tells the dribbler where their head and eyes should be as they dribble and I usually add **NEXT PASS** after this

- **LEFT HAND/RIGHT HAND** – tells the player which hand to dribble with away from the defensive player usually to the outside of the court

- **GO HARD** – I prefer this to "ALL THE WAY" which is a very popular and I might add selfish command that far too many coaches use. Basically, by telling a player to go all the way they have a full green light to shoot the ball and disregard any of their teammates who may be in a far better position. **GO HARD** is far better as you want the player to attack the basket and if the opportunity to shoot is there then great if not, they can pass

- **ALL CLEAR** – this lets the player with the ball know that they have a break on the defence and can drive in for a smooth layup with no need to rush the shot

- **LAYUP** – always encourage your players to shoot a layup rather than stop and let the defensive player catch them and put them under pressure on the shot

- **BOARDS** – a simple key word to help players remember to rebound. You can also isolate this to one or two players that are the taller players of the team by adding their name to the **BOARDS** call

- **SNAKES** – our end line play close to our basket. I will also use the word **GO** and we train them not to move until I say **GO** otherwise anxious young players will cut far too early and end up standing in the key with their defensive opponent and clogging the key so their teammates will have little chance to get a close to the basket shot

- **LINE (Side-line)** – our side ball play. Make sure players start back towards the middle of the court near to the split line to create space to lead into and wait for the coach to yell **GO**

- **LINE (Baseline)** – our baseline out of bounds play near our basket we introduce this to older beginners once they gain some playing experience that gives multiple options to score

- **MOTION** – a very simple man to man defensive offence we teach once players are older and have just passed the beginner stage

- **SHOOT IT** – sounds strange to add this one in but some players forget to shoot the ball at times, so there is nothing wrong with the coach telling them to

- **GREAT PASS** (Players Name) – always praise the passer in most situations as passing will be the foundation for great teamwork

- **GOOD JOB** (Players Name) – always reward a player with this praise, it tells them that what they did was important to our team

- **GREAT TEAM BASKETBALL** (YOUR TEAM'S NAME) – when the team puts together a really good play phase where multiple players are involved that leads to a score or just a great shot let the team know

Defence

- **MATCH UP** – you would think that players do this automatically but believe me coach it will take some time before this becomes a habit of everyone on the team picking up an opposition player

- **TOUCH** – this really helps your players stay with the opposition player they're supposed to be guarding and if there touching them, not fouling them then this process is far easier for beginner players to understand. If you're actually touching the opposition player then you're staying with them which is what we want from our defence.

- **STANCE** – this reminds the players that they need to get into a defensive stance to play good defence

- **NUMBERS** – this lets the player tell you and each other who they are guarding

- **COVER/SAFETY** (PLAYERS NAME) – I always have one player who is responsible for defensive safety which means defending the basket as our last line of defence

- **HELP** – a player has beaten the player guarding the ball and will need assistance from their teammates to stop an easy shot. This will take a little time to develop but well worth using as you will need it throughout your coaching at every level of basketball

- **HE-ME-BASKET** – you will use this quite a lot in the beginning and then you will pick out individuals who need help in this area of their game

- **SHE-ME-BASKET** – use this one when coaching girls asking for the same position on defence that **HE-ME-BASKET** does

- **STOP BALL** – this is a must as hard driving players will tear up your defence and create easy opportunities to score. The quicker you slow or stop the driving player the easier it will be for everyone to pick up a player and get back to defend your basket

- **CHASE BACK** – at times you will need your players to chase back especially when the opposition is attacking the basket and there is nobody there to stop them

- **SMOTHER** – this encourages the player to keep their hands up and over the offensive player with the ball not allowing an easy shot or pass. I stay away from just saying "HANDS UP" as players could be too far away from the ball to make any impact and putting hands in the air will not help the situation if they're not close enough to their opponent

- **BACK** – I would hope you use this far more than chase back. It alerts all the team that the opposition now has possession of the ball and we need to get back on defence

- **PUSH IT LEFT/RIGHT** – this tells the defensive player to force the dribbler to their off-hand and will be a valuable skill that will pay great dividends for your team once players are skilled enough to do this.

- **THREE STEPS BACK** – this is to counter both side ball and end line out of bounds plays (make sure they're not doing this if an opponent is close to the basket). You will find that once you start running the plays in this book, most if not all teams you play against will adopt them also. By having players drop back a few steps you will counter the offensive players making easy cuts for shots without pressure.

- **BOARDS** – the same key word used in the offence but far more important here as it will give your opponent far more scoring opportunities

- **GOOD JOB** (PLAYERS NAME) – you may want to use this one a little more to encourage players to become good defenders. It is far easier to become a great defender in a short period of time than it is to be a great offensive player.

Now being the creative beings, that we humans are I am sure you will find a few words not listed here that suit both you and your team. These are a great start and I seldom use any more than the ones listed when communicating with players on court. You will favour some words over others but the most important thing is to constantly use them at training and these will flow effortless and easily during the game.

After a few games, you will certainly have a far better idea of where your team stands in relation to general skills and teamwork. With the introduction of simple plays there will be a lot more to talk about, especially if things were lacking in our last game that could be mentioned, along with the good things we did. As a matter of fact, I would stroke the player's ego with the great things we did then hit them with things we need to avoid. When you tell them how wonderful they are, they will always be attentive to anything you will say after that. You will certainly be using many of the things from that first speech but the players need you to advance them through the various levels they need to develop as individuals and as a team.

Speech Samples
After your initial hello and how are you, you can get straight into what you need the players to do. They will be on a steep learning curve but after a few games won't suffer the same feelings they did before the first game and will have a better understanding of basic rules and with a few training sessions under their belts a better idea of what you want them to do.

"Okay guys remember our 3 basic rules."

- **"Look after the ball"** – Have your players demonstrate pivoting and protecting the ball. Fire questions at them. Who do I look at before I pass the ball to a teammate? Answer "the defence."

- **"Shoot good shots"** – A player must know what a good shot is. You must discourage shooting from long range and definitely no three-point shots. I will bench players for poor shots sending a message that these types of shots are bad for the team. Encourage every player to shoot layups rather than stopping to shoot set shots when they are ahead of the defence. Go through the shot action with them to reinforce good habits.

- **"Hustle with the feet on defence"** – Young players are prone to get into foul trouble, by reaching and hacking, at anyone with the ball. Moving the feet and maintaining position will, one helps your players keep opposition scores lower and two, keep tumbles and injuries down to a minimum. Get your players to show you the defensive stance and a few drop step slides and then the **SMOTHER** when their player has the ball close to the basket.

"Boys/Girls or Team last game we played it was really good the way we stayed with our players on defence and SMOTHERED most of the time. I think we can pass the ball a little stronger and SPLIT a little faster. We took some great shots but don't you think we could do even better if we remember the panic and rushed shots will never score many baskets so let's not get too excited when we are taking shots." This is a small example of what I may say at training or include in a pre-game address and other things I use quite often are questions, as it makes kids a little more thoughtful with their actions. I like to use **"is it important?"** in most of the questions I ask and remember coaches if it isn't important to you it certainly will not be important to the players you work with.

Example Questions – preceded by "Is it important…"

- **"we keep our head up when we dribble and why?"**
- **"you pass the ball forward to an open teammate?"**
- **"to SPLIT when we get the rebound after they shoot and how fast?"**
- **"to pass strong or soft?"**
- **"to make more bounce passes when the defence is taller?"**

- "fake a pass to make a pass?"
- "to rebound strong and above your head with both hands?"
- "get back quickly on defence?"
- "pick up the same player on defence?"
- "we SMOTHER when they are close enough to shoot?"
- "someone COVERs and plays SAFETY every time they have the ball?"
- "STOP THE BALL when they are attacking?"

Now with some of these questions I get the players to simulate (pretend in their language) the actions I want. Kids are great because they want to get better and even though this may be a little confusing to some, keep planting the seeds of greatness in them and they will surprise and delight you. You can use these questions as a guide and I am sure you will make adjustments to suit your team and add a few statements and let the players know what is important to you.

Example Statements

- "Play smart and have fun"
- "We are wearing the (colour of your uniform) uniforms, make sure you pass to your teammates wearing the (colour of your uniform) uniform"
- "Keep your eyes up and see the court every time you have the ball and look towards the basket"
- "Make sure your passes are strong and to a teammate and not lobbed in the air for anyone to get the ball"
- "Get close on the SMOTHER and make sure it is really hard for them to shoot a good shot"

As you can see the statements are simple and on point and I am sure you will have a few favourites you will use regularly and without a doubt have many that are simple and help get your message across.

Here is checklist of things to do and focus on during the game.

1. **Keep instructions simple and clear coach. USE KEY WORDS**

2. **Make regular substitutions** – this will keep your players motivated as all players love to be on the court. With players only on for short periods of time there should be far more intensity in your teams play and a great opportunity to teach as they come to and from the bench.

3. **Praise the passer** far more than the player who makes the basket. Most players get a buzz from scoring, yet to promote good teamwork and get more players involved in the game "passing is the key".

4. **Develop as many players as you can**, it is so easy to leave it up to your star player/players to help you win the game. Encourage your players to try new things, to really get involved in the game. This has been a real plus for my club as we tend to improve everyone and many teams, we play against rely on one or two players who generally ignore their teammates.

5. **Give your players responsibility**. They must guard their player, they must look after the ball, they must take good shots, learn from their mistakes and stay away as much as possible from constantly repeating simple ones, encourage and support their teammates, as this is all part of being in a team.

6. **Promote team spirit as much as possible**. A simple thing is to get players to high-five each other coming to and from the court on substitutions. Have players on the bench cheer on the good things their teammates do during the game. Criticism of teammates cannot be tolerated in any shape or form. We all make mistakes and it is the understanding of this that will help your players be far more tolerant. An important life skill that can be started by a simple game of basketball.

7. **Promote communication**. As a player subs in for another have them ask them which player they have to guard. When fouls shots are being taken, call over the two players not involved and keep giving instructions based on the **KEY WORD** system, especially after they get past the beginner stage.

8. **Coach the players who are sitting on the bench** with things you like that are happening on the court, even if it is the opposition players doing the

good things. Players need examples to follow and if it isn't someone on your team setting it then point out the other teams' good play as something we should try and replicate.

TIME OUTS, HALF TIME AND POST GAME ADDRESS TIPS

During the game the only time you will be able to address the whole team will be time outs and the half time break. Now the number of time outs will vary between two, three and four depending on the rules of your competition. Time outs last only one minute or so, depending on the diligence of the referees and in this small period of time you can achieve a great deal. With fresh instructions, your team can come back out and reverse a negative situation, and if playing well you may keep the momentum going with positive feedback. If used at the right time it can also become an effective lesson teaching players' skill and concepts, we cover at training sessions, a brief one at that, where lessons learnt at training can be re enforced. **KEY WORDS** will play a big part in your time outs and the whole teaching process is linked to the constant repetition and drilling of these vital words.

Key Points for effective time outs

• Allow your players to sit and get a drink for the first 10 to 15 seconds. During this time know exactly what you need to say in the simplest terms that your players will understand. Some coaches make small notes during the game to help guide their time outs, half time and post-match talks, along with providing a guide to things you will need to work on at training.

• You must get your players attention! You get 45 seconds to impart your wisdom and send them back out there. I have a small attention-grabbing statement "give me your ears and eyes". What you find with most young players is that they hear everything you say, but sometimes have a hard time listening. As the coach at trainings and games you can help them with two skills that will serve them well throughout life listening and concentration. I have had countless parents come up to me and thank me that their son/daughter is doing so much better in school, since they have starting playing basketball. I always feel great pride when hearing this, as I truly believe we as coaches, can teach kids life skills far beyond the simple game of putting the leather ball through an iron hoop.

- Try not to generalise too much. Some coaches do this giving the players a run-down of how bad things are going and can waste the whole time out this way. Or you can go the other way, telling them how wonderful they are and it's great to be positive and encouraging, yet I still feel it's a valuable time to teach. I will usually give a quick overview of what is good first. Always lead with what the teams doing well (everyone loves to be praised and encouraged) as this will get the players attention, rather than focusing on the negative things first. The next step is to hit them with what we need to change and then give clear instructions to each of the players going back on the court. Remember, tell players what you want from them as the subconscious mind does not understand a negative. Refrain from using words such as **'don't'** and **'can't'**, these will only encourage your players do the exact opposite. I cannot stress this point enough! I use this technique regardless of the level of basketball I am coaching from the beginner to elite player.

Following these points will certainly help your team perform better and will build respect for you as the team leader. Now that you have a handle on how the time out will be structured the next important thing to know is when to actually call them. A game of basketball will throw up so many challenges and situations. Time outs should be used wisely as they can have a dramatic effect on the performance of your team and the outcome of a game. If you only need to make a point to one or two of your players, then make a substitution rather than waste a time out. Your message will be far more effective to these players as they will be eager to get back into the game.

Good times to call time outs

- The opposition has jumped you and you find your team is rattled and constantly making mistakes. Even if it's a few minutes into the game you have to settle the team down or at the very least make several substitutions to make sure the game doesn't spiral so far, away that players get dejected.

Now sometimes the opposition are just too strong, tall, athletic and far more skilful and at the very least the time out will slow their scoring and give you an opportunity to focus on simple things to control the ball and slow down their run.

- The game is congested, with too many players surrounding the ball and neither team is really achieving much. A good time here to emphasise the **SPLIT** and create space for your team to play.

- When your team has a big lead and you want to help the opposition out by taking some of the pressure off them coming down the court.

- You have limited or no subs and the players need a break to keep them as fresh as possible to be competitive. If your team has momentum and is playing well, hold off for as long as you can, before calling the time out. Players seldom get tired when everything is working well and the game has a good rhythm and flow, and you have a good lead. Time outs are limited though and make sure you use them wisely and well-spaced to give players a decent time to recover.

- Last minute situations to make the players aware of what is needed to score or advance the ball down the floor, to know who to pick up on defence and just to focus on all our training and remain alert.

- To help an injured player recover and get them back into the game after some minor treatment, especially if you have some momentum and they have been important to this.

- The team has just made a fantastic play, possibly using all players to create a basket. If you have plenty of time outs to spare, use one to praise all players and hold it up as an example of how we want to play. These are priceless time outs that really build and bind your teamwork and spirit. This also sends a strong message to the players that passing is a key to great team basketball.

- Calling a time out towards the end of the game to give your post-match address rather than waiting until the end of the game. I have often done this if I have important points that need to be addressed, rather than at the end of the game, when young tired bodies are distracted and wanting to head off.

- Call a time out to teach certain plays or concepts you have been working on in training. – Take every opportunity to give them positive messages and correction of bad habits, silly decisions and poor play. I preach playing winning basketball, not winning games at every opportunity.

Strategy and Tactics

Very early on in your team's humble beginnings, you will be getting to know what your team can and can't do. At this stage **KEY WORDS** and concentrating on simple fundamentals will be the main focus and all the side really needs. As the season rolls on and the players understand most of the rules and how the game functions and their role as players on a team, you may need to implement something extra and possibly expand on **KEY WORDS** and basic plays. There will be times where you will need simple game tactics and strategy to help your team perform better. This will also build respect from your players and parents and even the opposition that you indeed are a coaching genius or at the very least mildly competent.

There will often be times when players will be confused about the rules and yet some kids will amaze you as they will quickly pick up what they need to do, and if your team is very athletic, you could have a great first game and a very easy victory. On the other side though, you may have kids who struggle with simple concepts along with their coordination and the team may get beaten quite badly or the game could be close and exciting and stressful for you the coach and the parents.

Applying effective pressure

Once your team has grasped the concept of, **HE/SHE-ME-BASKET** defensive principles you can now look to apply a little more pressure to opposing teams. Don't guard the player passing in from out of bounds. Have the player guarding the inbounds passer back off and play a **SAFETY** role. This allows the four players to play the opposition players really tight as there is a teammate behind to help them if their player gets away from them. It is here you can apply the concept of **COVER** defence to further educate your players. **COVER** defence is an important concept for players to learn as it will become the last line in your defence yet the first thought in applying defensive pressure and any offensive structure your team eventually adopts. I have covered this in more detail in the defensive section but it is definitely worth repeating and adopting.

COURT TIME

I have an equal court time policy with every team I coach during the regular season, and try and stick to this as much as I possibly can. I will however in close games go with the kids who are performing well on the day for the final few minutes. Sometimes the referees let the game go and make few calls so this can be a real challenge at times as you may need players to foul to get players in the game so long as it doesn't disadvantage your team too much. Blow-out games give you an opportunity to add some extra playing time for the kids who are struggling a little with their skills and concepts. In the tougher matches, you can swing slightly the other way. At times, I have kept certain players in the game for extended periods of time due to the fact they may be the only player that can match a tall or very talented athlete and will sub them when the opposing coach subs.

Over the course of the season I am very mindful of court time and for most teams it will usually even out by the seasons end with everyone sharing the minutes on court. It is always much easier though if your team is well balanced with a few bigger players to compliment the smaller and average height players. Come finals times everyone definitely plays but we do give ourselves the best opportunity to take home a trophy for our efforts over the course of a season. My club doesn't have individual awards or participation trophies at an awards night at the end of a season as I prefer players play for the club and their team and if we win a trophy at the end of the season everyone contributed. My club has had a very successful run the last few seasons with approximately 70% of our teams seeing post season action and we have between 40 and 50% playing off in the final game of the season. This is due to having a well-tested system but also grounding our players with many of the principals taught in this book by all our coaches.

CREATIVE COACHING TIPS WHEN YOU'RE UP OR DOWN

What to do when you're 15 – 20 points up

As a coach you will have times when your team is stronger than the opposition or just hits a purple patch and builds quite a lead a short time into the game. Some coaches look at this situation where the team is cruising and switch off, preferring to just make substitutions or worse try and totally crush the opposing team. Crushing an opposition team and not letting them score or even get shots up does little for the game of basketball or keeping kids interested in playing the sport. We all have an obligation, especially at the beginner level to help kids enjoy the game and keep playing regardless of whether they play for your team or the opposition.

Now some competitions have mercy rules to help blow-out situations but it really is the responsibility of the coach and the discipline of the players. I am always looking for creative ways in which to help my players improve their game. Here are a few ideas and I'm sure as you get more into coaching you will find many creative ways in which to challenge your players and yet not send the opposition home feeling terrible after getting smashed.

- Back your defence up to the halfway line once you're 15 points up and to the three-point line once the margin hits 20. You have to demand all the players do this and it may take several tries and some players will forget and push forward and pressure. Some young players find it hard to concentrate and this is a golden opportunity to help them focus and stay disciplined. Players who don't get back are substituted immediately. This may seem a little harsh but I never leave a player off too long as a matter of fact the very next opportunity to substitute will see them back on the court a far more disciplined player. The bench is a motivating factor as all players want to be on the court. If they repeat the episode of pressuring up the court, then another quick substitution will ram home the message.

- If your players have backed off and are still stealing the ball at will and the opposition cannot get any shots up, I then have my players in this situation play hands on shorts defence (well near shorts rather than actually grab them). Now you might think this is belittling to an opposition team, having been on the end of several severe beatings I can tell you that your players will appreciate any chance to score a basket. With hands on shorts defence your players are still working on a vital fundamental which player's especially young ones have a hard time with which is footwork. Even though we are playing hands on shorts, I demand players stay between the player they are guarding and the basket and can only raise them after the shot goes up. Under no circumstances are they to steal the ball. I would substitute players breaking this rule under the same guidelines as the previous backing up on defence rule. There is nothing worse than a team not scoring a basket it is a very sad and hollow feeling having nothing to show at the end of a game for all your teams' efforts. The exception to this is of course the score line reads 1 or 2 to 0 and I am not suggesting you give the game away if very little scoring has taken place for either team.

- One of the hardest parts of the game to teach is the use of the opposite hand. When your team has a decent lead in a game make them play with only the opposite hand. At this point you have got to pose the question of what will your side really get out of a crushing victory other than some layup practice. Your players will resist playing with their non-dominant hand and again I would implement the quick substitution rule. Kids are amazing how quickly they pick things up and it will be quite challenging to them to force their brain to cope with this shift from the normal dominant strong hand way of playing.

- A simple way to see they are actually playing with their non-dominant hand is the use of a sweat band on their opposite hands. Have your players bring these to the games where there are clear differences in the ability of both teams based on a previous meeting. As I continually preach to any players I coach, become a weapon a two-sided player, not a half player. The ability to use both sides of the body can never be understated and this can also be done at training.

- Every player on the team must score before anyone can score multiple goals. This is extremely challenging to your players as most teams usually have only two or three dominant scorers. You will have a lot of fun watching your players resist the urge to score knowing that they have to help their teammates get a basket. It takes a fair amount of self-discipline to give up making an easy basket to help a teammate get the same result. You as the coach will also have to help the players disguise the fact that we are trying to help a particular player score the next hoop. It's another simple way to give your team a focus when the game is basically over so far as a result is concerned, in the first half. Now put a time limit on this if it is taking forever or make it an, every second play option if you're down to the last player to score option.

- Make your team play a modified game. Now the previous points do this to some degree yet you can still take this a little further by promoting different skills with various players on your team. I will often ban the dribble if I believe players are ignoring each other in making a forward pass or if our previous game was an over use of the dribble. I would also put this rule in to help these young players get vital practice in passing, leading and cutting. It really is a great way to promote teamwork and get every player involved on the offensive end.

Having different rules for each player I find is really productive once you get to know your team and their strengths and weaknesses. Remember to keep it simple and just give each player one or two easy things to work on. Here are a few examples I am sure with some imagination you can add a few extra.

1. **No dribble at all.**

2. **Only One, Two or three dribbles then you must pass.**

3. **Throw chest, bounce or overhead passes only.**

4. **You must dribble (helpful for players who are reluctant to dribble).**

5. **Play with opposite hand only.**

6. **You must fake before making a pass or drive.**

7. **All the defensive rules above.**

8. **Shoot shots outside the key if the other team gives you easy inside shots.**

9. **Three to Five seconds and you must move the ball on regardless if you are dribbling.**

There will be times when some of the players on your team will barely be involved in the game. They will be timid or placid kids who are just happy to be on the team or they may have a slight disability. Whatever the reason for most parts of the game they will run from free throw line to free throw line and hardly touch the ball or pick up a player. With this type of player, I will actually encourage them to try and steal the ball from their opponent or at least try and touch it. With some players, you have to encourage them to be close enough to the opposition to almost foul and I want them to get used to being physical but fair. I never would ask a player to go out and hit an opposition player as this a very cowardly act that should never be encouraged or tolerated on any basketball court. It is important however, to get your players used to physical contact. The nature of playing a sport in a confined area will have players constantly coming into contact throughout the game and at training.

What to do when you're 15 -20 points down
It is sad to see a once robust coach at the start of a game suddenly sit down and get very quiet once their team is down by quite a considerable margin. I am a firm believer in coaching out the game regardless of the scoreboard. It is when the chips are down that your team really needs your support and more importantly your full focus and attention. A team will often feed off their coach and you being the leader will need to keep them motivated especially when things aren't going so well. This is the most challenging part of coaching and not something to fear or dread as it happens to the best of coaches at some stage. The most important thing you can do as the coach is just keep coaching. It will

be a real test of character for your team and for you, and some coaches find it hard to cope especially when things have been going really well for the best part of the season.

It is during this time that I start to look for players who are not hanging their heads and praise them for this. I also point out the things that the opposition are doing really well and use this as an example of what I would like players from our team to be doing. It is a great teaching point praising an opposition players as examples of how you would like your players to play and it also sends the message that they are not the enemy, but sometimes really good teachers, although this is hard to really grasp when you're getting thrashed. It also breeds respect for the opposition teams and it is important to show your players that they just like us are learning the game and experiencing the highs and lows of competition. At times your team may have several of these games in a row or just be like several of my young teams that are placed in a grade that is beyond their skill and physical level.

Faced with this situation, players can become very passive and feel defeated before they even step on the court, or some players won't care too much and get very sloppy with their general play, allowing their concentration to slip and repeat basic mistakes over and over. I never really mind getting beaten if I see players putting in an effort, or at the very least are trying to play winning basketball and are working on the things they have been taught at training. It's a great life lesson also that there will be times in life that it will be hard and things don't always go your way. Helping players overcome this is one of the hardest parts of coaching a team and will be a great test for not just the players but also the coach and parents. It is important to keep teaching the essential basic skills and simple structures and trust in this and keep driving this repetition until you start to see small patches of winning basketball. Use the quick sub technique to help keep players focused and coach keep coaching, hang tough and in the immortal words of Sir Winston Churchill **"NEVER EVER GIVE UP."**

FURTHER COACHING TIPS

I heard a really great quote once, not sure who the author was but I think its pure gold – **"There is no secret to success; you just do small things in a successful way every day."** What a great philosophy to adopt in your coaching and in your life and small victories every day will mount up over time into great success overall. Now you may not be coaching the team or working with the players every day but you can help them have small successes every training session and game. This will slowly build over time and begin to show itself in all games. It is really hard to gauge sometimes how much a player or team has improved, especially if you're not doing so well in your current season until you see them up against other kids who may just be starting to play and realise, they have made steady progress.

Quick Substitution Technique

I am always trying different techniques and I constantly experiment to find anything to help the team perform better. With a few teams, mistakes can spiral into a never-ending sea of turnovers and be a great source of frustration to some players, most parents and you the coach. At times, you will have to take measures to help educate your players. I normally substitute a player if they make two very quick mistakes, just to settle them down and make them get refocused and then get them back in the game as soon as possible. In the past I have implemented a quick substitution policy with several teams, just to help players become a little more thoughtful with their actions. This is done in a gentle manner and you are guiding them to help make themselves and the team better and to teach them responsibility for their actions. With beginners you can do this and keep them next to you and explain exactly what you want from them and send them back in next sub.

Quick Subs Checklist

- Throwing the ball straight to the opposition multiple times. Here, it is important for you to tell the player to not get too excited and make sure they pass to the players wearing our uniforms. Have them pivot and protect the ball and explain they have plenty of time to pass. They can throw fake passes and dribble if there is nobody free to pass to. Passing strength may be a big problem here so some extra push-ups at training will help them build some strength.

- Not picking a player up on defence. This poor habit will hurt the team, so explain that we spend over half the game playing defence. Have an assistant coach, teammate, parent or older sibling who is on or near the bench pretend to be the player they're guarding and have them stay with them while sliding backwards in a good defensive position.

- Watching the opposition shoot the ball on consecutive plays. Explain that it is important to keep playing defence until we get the ball and you must **SMOTHER** the ball whenever it is close to the opposing teams' basket.

Either you hold a ball or a teammate in a shooting action and have the player **SMOTHER** the ball in a straight up position and they can jump a little providing they keep their hands high and close together.

- Constantly travelling or double dribbling. Nothing will have teammates not passing to certain players who travel or double dribble every time they have the ball. It is really important to help kids break poor habits as quickly as possible, such as getting too excited and running with the ball or forgetting to pass after they pick up their dribble. It is simple with a few small demonstrations and simulations to promote the good habits.

- Dribbling with your head down. Explain to the young player that this habit really hurts the team and can cost us chances to score. Then pose to the player themselves that if they were out in front wouldn't they expect their teammate to pass the ball forward to them. Have them simulate heads up dribble by dribbling down to the end line and back and if this was successful then send the player back in as fast as possible.

- Not making the next open forward pass. This is a quick sub where a quick explanation is all that is needed and ask the question "if you're in front of the ball and open would you expect your teammate to pass the ball?" The answer you will always get is a very firm yes of course coach and so you just push the same point to the young player.

- Shooting a few really poor shots. A simple process of asking the player what is a good shot along the lines of **1)** Is rushing the shot, okay **2)** Shooting too far out **3)** Trying to shoot over a far bigger player in a decent guarding position **4)** Slamming layups hard into the backboard giving the shot absolutely no chance to go in **5)** Silly shots where you don't look at the basket and just fling the ball over head. Coach you simply say "look can you shoot a good shot or do I have to make this quick sub again and go back over all this again" they will nod their head yes and affirm they will do the right thing by themselves and the team and you pat them on the back and say, "I know you will do the right thing out there." Hopefully you don't have to repeat this sub too many times and it will usually be only for a few players, unless you have a totally selfish team that ignores passing altogether. In this case, you may need to sub frequently for ignoring open teammates until it registers with the players that this is a team game we are playing.

- Standing around and not rebounding. Similar to watching players shoot it is important that young players learn to play above their head and especially if they're bigger kids you need them to get our team rebounds. I usually appeal to the young players scoring ego here and ask them, "Would they like to shoot more baskets?" Their eyes light up as they answer yes and it is here you coax them into getting closer to the basket and raising their hands. I will usually throw a ball in the air here and have them tear the ball out of the air and bring it to their chin, then have them bring it up again in a mini-shooting action. When the player goes back into the game, try and focus a little attention on them by calling their name to rebound, when shots go up. A simple **KEY WORD** here is **BOARDS** Simon, **BOARDS** Joan, **BOARDS** Mark or **BOARDS** Sophie and repeat this at training so they understand that **BOARDS** means rebound. Now quite a few coaches will yell out rebound, so I prefer a word that our players will react to and not everyone on the court.

- Back-chatting and questioning the referees. I will not tolerate young players questioning umpires for missed or poor calls as their job is to concentrate on actually playing the game, not refereeing the game. This will not be a major problem for really young kids but there will be the odd time from older beginner players who may have watched older siblings play and think they know about every rule and their official interpretation. Now it can be frustrating for everyone when the officials are inexperienced, but the referees are the coach's responsibility to ask polite questions when the need arises. As soon as a player exhibits this poor behaviour it is a simple sub and a few questions about what their role is out on the court, to play or to referee. Once they realise that they may not get back into the game they quickly understand that you are not happy with this behaviour and they go back on the floor with a pat on the back to relax and just play.

- Arguing with teammates or you, the coach. An absolute no brainer coach and it will come back to our team rules of simple respect for everyone in the team. This shouldn't be a big problem with really young children but you may have the odd child with behaviour issues outside the team and these will have to be handled with patience and fair and firm discipline.

- Hurting players from the opposition with rough play. Nobody wants to see young children hurt playing sport or anyone for that matter. If I see players being unduly rough with the opposition players, I get them straight out of the game and quickly question why they are behaving this way. I ask them to be careful when they are playing and curb a little of that aggression as we are all here to enjoy the game and to play with a little more care, when they get back out on the court. Boys can get a little boisterous along with a few girls at times and a quick sub, a drink and a short period to settle them down is usually all that is needed. These players are the exact opposite to the ones who will not venture anywhere near the ball and it's a matter of finding the balance of controlled aggression to the ball as opposed to the player. Basketball is a contact game but this should always be fair contact in pursuit of the ball.

- Players wanting to coach the team. This will seldom happen but occasionally there will be a young player with a little too much to say and will start wanting to control the team and place themselves above the coach and the rest of their teammates. Similar to talking to referees and arguing with teammates, a quick sub and a subtle word to settle down and concentrate on playing which is all a player ever really has to do.

Now when you quick sub the young player out, you must speak to them about correcting the necessary behaviour or skill, then get them straight back in hopefully in a better state of mind and focus. I am always experimenting with various methods and I have used the quick sub method, which is really just another teaching tool in your coaching arsenal, to great effect, but it must be done in tandem with getting the player back in the game while the message is fresh as quickly as possible. You must remember that this could be interpreted as a very drastic step to take in the education of your players and my main reason is to make players a little more thoughtful. I would never do this for an entire season, only a short period is needed to make players become a little more focused.

If a player feels they will be subbed off for every mistake they will be far too scared to ever try anything, this is why it is important not to do it with absolute beginners in their first few games. In the pre-game talk, I tell them the reasons for doing this and it is to teach them to take more care and think through each play phase. I also use it to break bad habits which can undo everything we have worked on at training. I have on many occasions had great feedback from opposition parents for giving the kids really great direction which is heartening and I always let my parents know what I am doing so they don't get confused that I am not singling out their child.

- As you get more into your coaching you can individualise this by making it various rules for different players. Basketball is a game of habits and decisions and at times you the coach have to take action to help your players.

This is not few girls at times and a quick sub, a drink and a short period to settle them down is usually all that is needed. These players are the exact opposite to the ones who will not venture anywhere near the ball and it's a matter of finding the balance of controlled aggression to the ball as opposed to the player. Basketball is a contact game but this should always be fair contact in pursuit of the ball.

- Players wanting to coach the team. This will seldom happen but occasionally there will be a young player with a little too much to say and will start wanting to control the team and place themselves above the coach and the rest of their teammates. Similar to talking to referees and arguing with teammates, a quick sub and a subtle word to settle down and concentrate on playing which is all a player ever really has to do.

Now when you quick sub the young player out, you must speak to them about correcting the necessary behaviour or skill, then get them straight back in hopefully in a better state of mind and focus. I am always experimenting with various methods and I have used the quick sub method, which is really just another teaching tool in your coaching arsenal, to great effect, but it must be done in tandem with getting the player back in the game while the message is fresh as quickly as possible. You must remember that this could be interpreted as a very drastic step to take in the education of your players and my main reason is to make players a little more thoughtful. I would never do this for an entire season, only a short period is needed to make players become a little more focused.

If a player feels they will be subbed off for every mistake they will be far too scared to ever try anything, this is why it is important not to do it with absolute beginners in their first few games. In the pre-game talk, I tell them the reasons for doing this and it is to teach them to take more care and think through each play phase. I also use it to break bad habits which can undo everything we have worked on at training. I have on many occasions had great feedback from opposition parents for giving the kids really great direction which is heartening and I always let my parents know what I am doing so they don't get confused that I am not singling out their child.

As you get more into your coaching you can individualise this by making it various rules for different players. Basketball is a game of habits and decisions and at times you the coach have to take action to help your players. This is not always the most pleasant of tasks and yet it is invaluable to your team if a bad habit has been eliminated and replaced with a good one. Being part of a team, an individual player must take responsibility for their actions. Even at the beginner level you are working with, players must realise they are an important part in the overall group and the habits they form and the decisions they make will affect the overall performance of the side.

CHALLENGES AND OPPORTUNITIES OF COACHING

Challenges and opportunities are a part of life and coaching is no exception. I would like to say that everything you will do with your coaching will be a totally wonderful, positive experience that will bring absolute joy and satisfaction for all your efforts. In the world of fairy-tale basketball that could be the reality. You make all the right moves, your kids make all their shots, hit all their targets with their passes, play flawless man to man defence and win every game and take all before them including the championship trophy. The reality is everyone has bad days, teams have bad games, players take two steps forward and three steps back, sometimes you will totally out-play teams and shoot horribly, winning or losing a close one.

Now dealing with your team's performance will not be the only challenge, you will encounter as a coach. You must remember you are dealing with kids with different personalities, backgrounds and lifestyles and then they come as a package with their parents and guardians. Having coached so many teams over a long period of time has given me an array of experiences dealing with not only my own, but opposition players, parents, officials and the challenges that brings. I could probably write another book on this subject alone and yet I will list a few areas that could help you, after 28 years I have encountered more than my fair share of challenges.

Parents – Coaches, like it or not you will have to deal with parents and guardians if you are coaching their kids. I instruct my young coaches to get to know all the parents of the kids they're coaching, so when small challenges do arise you already have lines of communication open and I find most people are reasonable and work things out really quickly. The major lesson here is to build relationships with parents and keep communicating, after all we are here to help the kids get better and enjoy the game. A great way to get parents on your side is to have them involved in their own child's development as a basketball player by working with their kids on their skills, and they will also value you far more as a coach. With really ambitious parents it is worthwhile to point out that to master anything in life takes an incredible number of hours of dedicated training, so be supportive and it is a team game where every player deserves equal attention but you fully support their child.

Referees – Players and coaches make so many mistakes every game but most would never admit this yet a referee makes a couple and they are condemned by most at the game. Now don't get me wrong there are some outstanding officials and there are really poor ones and it can certainly test the most patient of coaches. Beginners will have a hard-enough time learning the rules, developing their skills and working with their teammates to really worry about the referees, but coaches can be challenged by decisions and non-decisions alike. It is important to note that refs make decisions based on the angle they are standing and not the angle you're viewing the game from. You will have a hard-enough time with your players than to worry about some calls that are not in your favour. The only time I will speak to the referees is if I feel they are letting too much contact go and it starts to get dangerous for the players. I have had players break their arms so it is important to protect the players when contact is getting out of control. In this instance always be respectful and polite and express your concerns about excessive contact that could result in serious injury. A few extra fouls that get called can quickly settle a game down so everyone can enjoy themselves.

CONCLUSION

I remember fondly the impact some of my coaches made on me especially my first coach, as without him I would never have discovered my love and passion for the game of basketball. I have seen first-hand the difference that coaches at our club make by really being involved in a positive way with the kids' development as players. To see parents out on the court playing with their kids and having an absolute ball, is part of what makes this a special game that can have such an impact. My experience with my own daughter Brodie is a testament to this and she's now forging her own coaching identity at our club, mentoring younger coaches as well.

It was such a great time for reflection as I delved into my memory banks drawing on so many training sessions and games to bring this book to a reality. I wanted to create a resource for the absolute novice coach and parent and also include some practical advice, by building a pathway for coaches and parents with some basketball experience, that would help give them the tools to develop both players and team.

The key word system of coaching beginners was such a quantum leap for me working at this level of basketball, I always felt that implementing it really gave me an unfair advantage over my opposition, especially if we faced teams with similar skill levels at the start of a season. By seasons end our team had improved so much that we were looking forward to moving up to stronger competition or even playing out of our age group to help further challenge the players. Now not every player and team perform to our high level of expectation and occasionally it really is hard to gauge exactly what the level of improvement has been, until we place them against the next group of beginners and realise how much they really have improved. It is then that I see the true value in the system and our training methods and take great pride in our coaches and players and their passion and love of the game of basketball.

What a privilege it has been working with kids, coaches and parents over the last 28 years. I really felt it was the right time to put my life's work into something that will make a difference and hopefully touch many people's lives. Bless all that have come on this journey with me over the years, (a special mention to my partner Sheryl) and the many more that will share my journey in the future.

I wish you the very best of success not just in basketball but in life, help kids dream big dreams and also remember to dream some big dreams yourself and do it with passion and purpose.

Coach Mark Anthony Walker

WHERE TO PLAY

There are many places to play basketball throughout Australia, Papua and New Zealand and all the major State and National Associations have information on where you can find a local club in which to play and are listed below. If you live in or around the inner South East Melbourne area in my home state of Victoria, you can play for my club the Central City Breakers Basketball Club which plays in the Hawthorn Basketball Competition and we cater for both beginners and experienced players. You can find a team to play with or start your own team with a group of friends. We also teach and mentor coaches for those that are interested in getting started on their own amazing journey.

Inner South East Melbourne
Central City Breakers
Telephone: 0416030562
Email: centralcitybreakers@gmail.com
Website: www.thebasketballedge.net

Basketball Australia
Telephone: +61 3 9847 2363
Email: info@basketball.net.au
Website: www.australia.basketball

Basketball Victoria
Telephone: (03) 9927 6666
Email: enquiries@basketballvictoria.com.au
Website: www.basketballvictoria.com.au

Basketball New South Wales
Telephone: (02) 8765 8555
Email: info@nswbasketball.net.au
Website: www.nswbasketball.net.au

Basketball Queensland
Telephone: (07) 3377 9100
Email: admin@basketballqld.net.au
Website: www.basketballqld.net.au

Basketball South Australia
Telephone: (08) 8345 8600
Email: admin@basketballsa.com.au
Website: www.basketballsa.com.au

Basketball Western Australia
Telephone: (08) 6272 0741
Email: admin@basketballwa.asn.au
Website: www.basketballwa.asn.au

Basketball Australian Capital Territory
Telephone: (02) 6253 3066
Email: admin@act.basketball.net.au
Website: www.act.basketball.net.au

Basketball Northern Territory
Telephone: 08) 8945 3761
Email: admin@nt.basketball.net.au
Website: www.nt.basketball.net.au

Basketball New Zealand
Phone: +64 4 498 5950
Email: bbnz@basketball.org.nz
Website: www.basketball.org.nz/

Basketball Papua New Guinea
Phone: +675 7326 3023
Email: admin@basketballpng.com
Website: http://www.bfpng.sportingpulse.net

BASKETBALL RULES FOR BEGINNERS

Game Purpose and Basics

To shoot the basketball through the Hoop as often as possible (at your team's scoring end! This will swap at halftime).

- Each time this happens, 2 points will be added to your Team's score.
- 3 Points will be awarded if the basketball is shot from outside the three-point line.
- 1 point will be awarded if the basket is shot from the free-throw line.

Each team has a maximum of 5 players on the court at any time. Substitutes are made by the Coach to replace players on the court. They are 'substituted' or 'subbed-off'. This can only be done at certain times in the game and the referee will let you know when it is OK. This can take place as often as the Coach likes.

The team who has control of the basketball is on OFFENCE. The team without the ball is on DEFENCE. Both parts of the game are equally important! Teams on defence are trying to stop the offence from shooting a hoop. The defence should always try to stay between the basket and the players they are guarding.

There are two ways for the ball to be moved up the court on offence - by 'dribbling' the ball, which is by bouncing the ball with ONE-HAND only on it, or by 'passing' it to another of your team members. Passing is a lot faster and ensures all team members enjoy the fun of the game.

While stationary (not passing or dribbling) the player holding the ball must always keep one of their feet on the floor, this is called the 'pivot' foot. Players can only lift their foot if they wish to dribble, pass or shoot the ball. The pivot foot can twist but must remain in contact with the floor and in the same place. If players move their foot/feet without dribbling, passing or shooting, they are penalized and the ball given to the other team, this is called 'travel'.

The ball must stay within the court of play (inside sidelines and baselines), otherwise it goes to the other team. No player may contact an opposition team member, this is called a 'foul'. If a foul takes place while a player is shooting for a basket, the shooter is given free shots from the free-throw line.

- If the basket (while being fouled) is scored, 2 points are awarded and 1 free-throw is taken.
- If the basket misses. 2 free-throws are given.
- If a player receives 5 fouls during a game, they must leave the court and can take no more part in the game.

Duration: generally, in junior competition a game is made up of two halves (usually 18 or 20 minutes each half).

Timeouts: A Coach can stop the game to talk to their players, usually a coach can call 3 time-outs depending on your competition over the duration (max. of 2 per half). When a timeout is called players must 'hurry' to the sideline to talk with their Coach.

Jump Ball: When 2 players get possession of the ball at the same time this is called a 'jump ball'. A jump ball starts the beginning of a game and after this a possession arrow is used alternating after each jump ball is called by the umpires.

Fouls and Violations

FOULS
Personal fouls: Personal fouls include any type of illegal physical contact.

· Hitting · Pushing · Slapping · Holding · Illegal pick/screen -- when an offensive player is moving. When an offensive player sticks out a limb and makes physical contact with a defender in an attempt to block the path of the defender.

Personal foul penalties: If a player is shooting while being fouled, then he gets two free throws if his shot doesn't go in, but only one free throw if his shot does go in.

- Three free throws are awarded if the player is fouled while shooting for a three-point goal and they miss their shot. If a player is fouled while shooting a three-point shot and makes it anyway, he is awarded one free throw. Thus, he could score four points on the play.
- Inbounds. If fouled while not shooting, the ball is given to the team the foul was committed upon. They get the ball at the nearest side or baseline, out of

bounds, and have 5 seconds to pass the ball onto the court.

- One & one. If the team committing the foul has seven or more fouls in the game, then the player who was fouled is awarded one free throw. If he makes his first shot, then he is awarded another free throw.
- Ten or more fouls. If the team committing the foul has ten or more fouls, then the fouled player receives two free throws.

Charging. An offensive foul that is committed when a player pushes or runs over a defensive player. The ball is given to the team that the foul was committed upon.

Blocking. Blocking is illegal personal contact resulting from a defender not establishing position in time to prevent an opponent's drive to the basket.

Flagrant foul. Violent contact with an opponent. This includes hitting, kicking, and punching. This type of foul results in free throws plus the offence retaining possession of the ball after the free throws.

Intentional foul. When a player makes physical contact with another player with no reasonable effort to steal the ball. It is a judgment call for the officials.

Technical foul. A player or a coach can commit this type of foul. It does not involve player contact or the ball but is instead about the 'manners' of the game. Foul language, obscenity, obscene gestures, and even arguing can be considered a technical foul, as can technical details regarding filling in the scorebook improperly or dunking during warm-ups.

VIOLATIONS

Walking/Traveling. Taking more than 'a step and a half' without dribbling the ball is traveling. Moving your pivot foot once you've stopped dribbling is traveling.

Carrying/palming. When a player dribbles the ball with his hand too far to the side of or, sometimes, even under the ball.

Double Dribble. Dribbling the ball with both hands on the ball at the same time or picking up the dribble and then dribbling again is a double dribble.

Held ball. Occasionally, two or more opposing players will gain possession of the ball at the same time. In order to avoid a prolonged and/or violent tussle, the referee stops the action and awards the ball to one team or the other on a rotating basis.

Backcourt violation. Once the offence has brought the ball across the mid-court line, they cannot go back across the line during possession. If they do, the ball is awarded to the other team to pass inbounds.

Time restrictions. A player passing the ball inbounds has five seconds to pass the ball. If he does not, then the ball is awarded to the other team. Other time restrictions include the rule that a player cannot have the ball for more than five seconds when being closely guarded and, in some states and levels, shot-clock restrictions requiring a team to attempt a shot within a given time frame.
For a PDF version of the rules go to the below online address. I am grateful to St Vincents for them putting this condensed simplified version together.

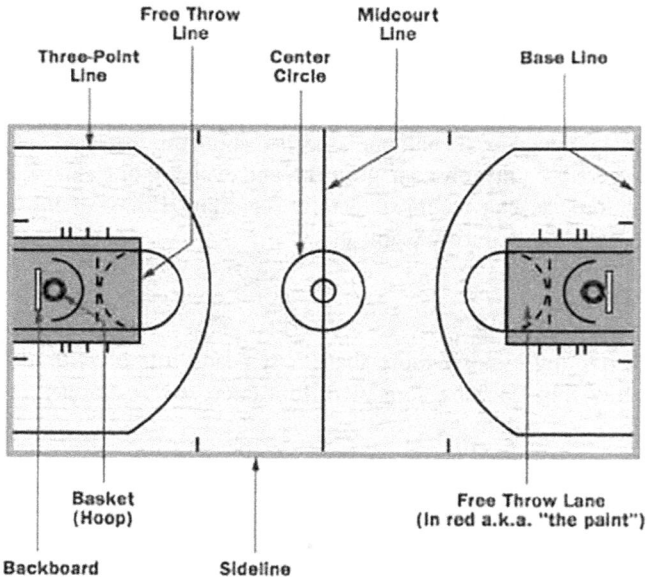

A BEGINNER'S GLOSSARY

TERM – DESCRIPTION

Backboard – The rectangular board from which the basketball ring is suspended.

Baseline – The out of bounds line behind the backboard at each end of the court.

Baseball Pass – A long one-handed pass thrown with the same method used to throw a baseball.

Basket – The goal. The basket has a hoop (metal ring) with a net hanging from it. The hoop is attached to a backboard 3.05m above the court surface.

Bounce Pass – A pass in which the ball is bounced once between the passer and the receiver.

Box Out – When a player turns or pivots into the path of another player who is attempting to rebound the ball.

Centre Circle – The circle in the middle of the basketball court.

Chest Pass – A two handed pass that is thrown from the chest.

Coach – The team's leader. The coach educates and develops players, determines player positions and applies strategy and plans for games.

Court – The playing area for basketball. The court is 28 metres long and 15 metres wide.

Defence – The act of retrieving the ball from the opposition or making it harder for the opposition to score.

Dribbling – Bouncing the ball with one hand. Either hand can be used but not both at the same time.

Fake – A misdirection ploy using body language and the ball to fool the opponent.

Field Goal – A shot that goes into the basket is a field goal except for free throws.

Forward – A playing position. There are two forwards on a team. Power Forward and Small Forward. These players are typically tall and powerful.

Foul – The act of illegally interfering with an opponent during play. Personal fouls and team fouls exist.

Free Throw – After being fouled by an opponent, a player gets one or more free throws from the free throw line.

Free Throw Line – A line on the court 5.8 meters from the baseline by which free throws are taken from.

Guard (Position) – A playing position. There are two guards on a team. Point Guard and Shooting Guard. These players are typically smaller and faster players who handle the ball well.

Guard (Defend) – An act of defence.

High Percentage Shot – A shot with a low degree of difficulty.

Inbound Pass – A pass made from outside the court of play to recommence the game.

Jump Ball – Used to commence play at the start of the game. The basketball is tossed into the air between two players by the referee and they jump to tip the ball to a teammate for possession.

Jump Stop – When a player stops by landing with two feet hitting the floor simultaneously. The player can then choose which foot to pivot on.

Layup – A type of basketball shot using the backboard as an aid to place the ball in the ring. A layup occurs when a player is near the ring and is generally considered a high percentage shot.

Low Percentage Shot – A shot with a high degree of difficulty.

Mid Court (Halfway) Line – The line that divides the court into two halves.

Offence – When your team has the ball you are playing offence.

Officials – The referees, score table officials and statisticians.

Out of Bounds – Outside the court of play.

Overhead Pass – A pass thrown from above the head with one or two hands.

Pass – One player throwing the ball to another player.

Personal Foul – The act of illegally interfering with an opponent during play. Each player can only foul personally five times in a game before being disqualified from further involvement in that game.

Pivot – When a player turns or pivots on one foot in order to change direction. The foot that they turn on is called the pivot foot. They can pivot in a forward direction (chest leading) or a reverse direction (back leading).

'Man to Man' Defence – A defensive strategy in which each defender guards a certain offensive player by standing as close to them as possible.

Possession – When a player has the ball in their hands they are in possession. A team is in possession when one of its players has the ball in their hands.

Rebound – When a shot hits the hoop or backboard and misses the basket players will compete to catch it. This is a rebound. Rebounds can be offensive or defensive.

Referee – An official who makes sure that the rules of the game are followed.

Shot – A type of shot attempting to get the basketball in the ring (jump shot, three-point shot, trick shot, corner shot).

Shoot – To shoot the basketball at the basket in an attempt to get it in the ring (entering from the top only).

Sideline – There are two sidelines, one on each side of the court.

Square Up – When a player turns their body toward the basket after catching the ball.

Stride Stop – When a player lands with a stride action, one foot touching the ground before the other. The first foot becomes the player's pivot foot.

Substitution – Interchanging of players from off court (substitute) with those on court (player). This is done during breaks in play.

Team Foul – Any personal foul becomes a team foul. If your team incurs more than 4 teams fouls per quarter the opposition shoots foul shots on any further fouls in that quarter (varies by competition).

Team Manager – The person responsible for looking after the players off court requirements and game day requirements. Not related to coaching.

Travelling – A violation occurring when a player walks or runs with the ball without dribbling.

Triple Threat Position – A stance that gives the offensive player the option to shoot, pass or dribble the ball.

Turn Over – An error that gives possession to the other team.

Violation – When a rule is broken.

Glossary provided by Basketball Australia and there are many terms used in basketball but these are great to get you started.

AUTHOR PROFILE
COACH MARK ANTHONY WALKER

Mark is an author, entrepreneur, basketball coach, and basketball instructor.

His career in basketball spans three decades. Having started from humble beginnings, Mark spent many years as an elite player. He then went on to spend more than 28 years as a professional coach and teacher, touching the lives of thousands of players in Australia and across the world.

Mark has coached a wide range of athletes that include male and female athletes, kids ages four through 19, young adults, seniors, deaf players, physically disabled players, and intellectually disabled players. Two of his proudest moments was coaching the first men's Paralympic team at the test games in Madrid, and winning the gold medal at the 1996 Paralympic Games in Atlanta, USA.

His love for the game and coaching wheelchair basketball is so strong that he played three years of competitive wheelchair basketball to improve his understanding of the mechanics of the game. That experience gave him invaluable insight into what it takes to teach basic skills. With this knowledge, he is able to demonstrate exactly what he requires from an athlete. He has purchased his own wheelchair and enjoys competing with other players.

Mark has coached and taught basketball clinics for both able-bodied and physically disabled players. The teams he has worked with include the Victorian Men's Wheelchair Basketball Team, the Australian Men's Team, the New Zealand National Team, Thailand National Wheelchair Men's Team, the South African Men's Wheelchair Basketball Team, the South Korean Wheelchair Basketball Federation, the Russian National Basketball Team, the Mexican Women's National Team, the Hong Kong National Team, The West Asian Basketball Team in Dubai and the Chennai Eagles Basketball team.

In addition to his coaching and instructing, Mark has built his own basketball club and business. The Central City Breakers started with just two teams and has grown to 92 teams. Many of his players have gone on to elite championship programs.

A student of the game, Mark maintains an extensive library of manuals, books, and more than 400 hours of videos about basketball and sports science. He is grateful to have worked with so many amazing people throughout his career and he is relentlessly pushing toward future successes and another Paralympic gold medal.

Mark Anthony Walker is the author of *Basketball for Beginners* and lives in Melbourne, Australia.

RECOMMENDED RESOURCES

RECOMMENDED RESOURCES

Motivational Inspirational Speaker

Looking for a speaker for your next event, training course, dinner or luncheon? Coach Mark Walker has built an impressive body of work in a long coaching career spanning over 25 years. Working with athletes from beginners to elite including players with various disabilities from intellectual, deaf and wheelchair basketball. Coaching isn't his only skill as Mark has built three major programs from the ground up and created history in Australia and several other countries. If your organisation needs inspiration and a different perspective on:

- Teamwork
- Team building
- Goal setting
- Motivation
- Leadership

- Creating a Core Covenant that is the backbone of successful Management
- Lessons from winning and defeat
- Create a lasting vision
- Mind Storming

Hear the positive and powerful messages through the language of sport and the truly inspiring story of the Australian Wheelchair Basketball Team at the Paralympic Games. The Power of a Dream that overcame all obstacles placed in our path on the way to a gold medal victory. With great video highlights of a truly remarkable team beating all the odds and making history and relive so many incredible moments that were truly life changing and empowering. I love sharing my story and insights, the challenges and the incredible highs and the life lessons from building a large body of work on every continent, working with an incredibly diverse group of people.

CONTACT
Email: goldmedalcoach@yahoo.com
Mobile: 0416030562
International: +61 416030562

Basketball Clinics & Camps

Coach Mark Walker is available to come to your Association and club and run some domestic coaching clinics and camps for your players, parents and coaches. Having coached thousands of domestic games building multiple programs over a long and fruitful career, Coach Walker will cover the topics relevant to the level of basketball players you're working with.

- Starting out with new players
- Working with boys and girls
- Establishing discipline
- Safety rules
- Essential basic skills
- Key Word concepts
- Training structure
- Basketball Drills

- Simple plays
- Game coaching and simple strategy
- Strength and conditioning
- Moving up to the next level
- Building a team and club
- Questions and answers session

Coach Walker will sign copies of his best-selling book **Basketball For Beginners** and every participant will have the chance to win a personal training session for their child or team.

CONTACT
Email: goldmedalcoach@yahoo.com
Mobile: 0416030562
International: +61 416030562

Global Basketball Community

Coming soon is a great new membership-based website that will be filled with great information, discounted products, resources and articles, interviews and blogs from around the **Global Basketball Community**.

- Basketball shoes and clothing
- Basketball training aids
- Basketball Books and DVD's
- Informative articles and blogs
- Games and Entertainment
- Competitions and Prizes
- Exclusive members

discounts on products and services
- Ask the Coach – Answers to your basketball questions
- Basketball Camps and Clinics information and special members deals
- Individual and Team training session offers from Coaches around the country

To help athletes with various disabilities there will be a comprehensive section that will include all of the above topics as well specialised information, services and equipment that is suited to the various athletes for their needs.

- Wheelchair Basketball
- Deaf Basketball
- Intellectual disability
- Modified preschool and early learning

Basketball is played in every country around the world so become a member of our **Global Basketball Community**. Join us now at
www.GlobalBasketballCommunity.com

Further Resources

There are many things both kids and their parents and coaches will need once kids start playing basketball. Our **Starter Packs** in the front of this book for players and coaches are a great start but eventually you will be looking for all sorts of products and services. A small word of caution, always do your research and due diligence before you purchase any product or services. Try things on, read reviews, ask your club, friends and family to help you make the best decisions.

Basketball Equipment and Supplies

Once kids start playing basketball there are great products you can get that will enhance their love of the game from trendy NBA clothes to many styles of shoes, balls, accessories, rings and backboard systems to suit every budget.

Retail Stores and Online Retailers

- Rebel Sport
- Kmart
- Amart
- Footlocker
- The Athletes Foot
- Nike retail and factory outlets
- Adidas retail and factory outlets
- Converse retail and factory outlets
- Under Armour
- EBay
- Amazon
- gumtree
- Truline
- Goalrilla Basketball
- MegaSlam Hoops Australia
- T&R Sports
- Spalding Australia
- First Ever
- Armando Sports
- Net World Sports
- Huffy Sports
- Basketball Republic
- Peak Sports
- National Basketball League NBL
- National Basketball Association NBA

Basketball Uniforms

Peter Fiddes has been a part of the basketball landscape for many years and I remember when I started my own club, I called into his shop and bought some blue and gold reversible singlets with iron on numbers. Twenty years later I have come full circle back to Fast Break Sports and fully endorse this supplier as he provides not just our sublimated uniforms, but a lot of team and basketball related products.

Contact Peter Fiddes at Fast Break Sports
Website: https://fastbreakbasketball.com.au/
Email: fiddes@fiddes.com.au
Phone: +61 3 9464 1721

General Health and Nutrition

Nutrition plays a part in all our lives and young growing bodies are no exception. Kids who have a balanced diet should have no problems getting all the vitamins they need from the foods they eat. Kids and adults who don't have well balanced diets and who are fussy eaters may need various supplements if their diet is inadequate.

- Sensational Kids
- Kids Health New Zealand
- Health Post
- Swisse
- Nutrition Australia
- Milo New Zealand
- Blackmores
- Chemist Warehouse
- iherb New Zealand
- Pharmacy Direct New Zealand
- Nutrition Warehouse
- Terry White Chemart
- Star Pharmacy

Physiotherapy

Injuries can happen at any time and not necessarily on the basketball court, at some point there could strains, sprains and parents who have been inactive for a while may also need the services of a good physiotherapist.

- Back in Motion Physiotherapy
- Domain Health Physiotherapy
- Premier Sports Medicine
- Physioplus
- Lifecare physio
- Activ Therapy

For a full list of Australian physiotherapy clinics go to
www.healthengine.com.au
To find a physiotherapist in New Zealand got **www.physiotherapy.org.nz**

Kids Banking
It's never too early to teach kids about saving and learning about money. A kid's bank account is often your child's first ever encounter with money concepts such as "saving" and "interest". All the banks listed have children's accounts and many with great interest for regular savers. A great life skill to obtain and retain.

- Bcu
- bankwest
- People's Choice Credit Union
- Bendigo Bank
- SUNCORP
- p&n Bank
- ANZ
- Westpac
- Commonwealth Bank
- ING

Team Building Activities
Teams of kids get together and train and play basketball games and for many they just leave it at that, which is okay if the kids are doing something healthy with mates. Over the years I have watched many parents do wonderful things to help build their kids and the teams they play for into really strong units. This has been enhanced by organising everything to play dates for new kids joining the side to outside activities that also help the parents and coaches' bond with each other.

- Family Friendly Restaurants – Hungry Jacks, McDonalds, La Porchetta, KFC, Red Rooster, TGI Fridays, Schnitz, Nando's, Subway, Trampoline, Ben and Jerry's, Wendy's, Cold Rock, Baskin-Robbins,
- Movies – Village, Hoyts, Dendy, Reading, Palace
- Fun Centres – depending on the age of the kids
- Barbecues – backyard cricket, fun games only limited by imagination
- A day at the park or beach depending on the season

Camera Suppliers

To capture great family memories and sporting moments these retailers both chain stores and online have a great range of products both still and video cameras.

- Ted's Cameras
- Harvey Norman
- JB HiFi
- Camera Warehouse
- Camera House
- Digi Direct
- Kogan

Gyms

I am a great believer in being a good healthy example to kids by staying in the best possible shape. Kids will follow the lead and examples of their parents and coaches and I fully encourage everyone to get and stay in shape to be at their best to spend quality time, with their family and team. Gyms have great programs and flexible hours so the most important element is the habit of using them. Gym chains are great in that you can use them when you travel and many also offer kids programs.

- Goodlife Heath Club
- Fitness First
- Snap Fitness
- F45 Gyms
- Jetts
- Plus Fitness
- Fernwood
- YMCA
- Anytime Fitness

People Movers

Growing families will need larger cars and SUV's have really been dominating this mode of travel for many years now. The safety factor for a family, along with the space, is a huge selling point for these cars and there are also crossover models that cover the in-between.

Toyota - Holden - Ford - Nissan - BMW - Mazda - Mercedes Benz - Volkswagen - Audi - Kia - Subaru - Hyundai - Honda - Suzuki - Jeep - Land Rover

www.ingramcontent.com/pod-product-compliance
Lightning Source LLC
Chambersburg PA
CBHW060019100426
42740CB00010B/1528

* 9 7 8 1 9 2 5 2 8 8 6 3 6 *